Fifty Years of Research on *Brazil*
A Photographic Journey

Mark J. Curran

Order this book online at www.trafford.com
or email orders@trafford.com

Most Trafford titles are also available at major online book retailers.

Printed in the United States of America.

ISBN: 978-1-4907-0837-9 (sc)
ISBN: 978-1-4907-0836-2 (e)

Library of Congress Control Number: 2013912904

Because of the dynamic nature of the Internet, any web addresses or links contained in this book may have changed
since publication and may no longer be valid. The views expressed in this work are solely those of the author and do not
necessarily reflect the views of the publisher, and the publisher hereby disclaims any responsibility for them.

All cover images are photos taken by the author, Mark J. Curran

Trafford rev. 02/05/2014

 www.trafford.com

North America & international
toll-free: 1 888 232 4444 (USA & Canada)
fax: 812 355 4082

Table of Contents

PREFACE

This book is meant to be a companion book to the recently published "A Portrait of Brazil in the Twentieth Century—The Universe of the 'Literatura de Cordel'". "Portrait" does indeed tell the story with all the story-poems, the sidebars of travel and my comments. I think, however, that there is a treasure of photographs taken over all those years from 1963 to 2013 that may be of interest and of value. Until now these photos have not been available to a public interested in Brazil and the "cordel," that is, other than presentations in the classroom at ASU and miscellaneous lectures to groups in Arizona and Colorado. What I have come to realize is that many photos of the poets, intellectuals interested in "cordel" and the actual scenes from the markets are not only of value for the "history" of those times, but more importantly, many of these scenes and people have passed from the scene. I hope this book fills in the gaps.

I will use markers to identify the photos, in some cases a single line identifying the scene. In many cases the markers will be followed by prose explaining in greater detail the person or place, the moment in time, and my impressions of it all. In Part I a primary source helpful to me in the text regarding the poets is the classic "A Bio-Bibliographic Dictionary of Popular Poets," ["Dicionário Biobibliográfico de Poetas Populares"] by Átila de Almeida and José Alves Sobrinho (Campina Grande, 2nd edition, 1990). It is the definitive source for biographical and bibliographical information on the poets of "old" "cordel" yet today. Átila was extremely kind to this writer in a visit in the 1990s shortly before his death after battling cancer. His private collection of "cordel," perhaps the best in Brazil, later became part of the library of the Regional University in Campina Grande, Paraíba State. Rare cordelian poems from that collection are part of my "História do Brasil em Cordel," "Retrato do Brasil em Cordel," and most recently, "Portrait." Once again, this is an important example of the hospitality that Brazilian intellectuals showed me once they were convinced I was a serious scholar and truly loved Brazilian "cordel."

In Part II the Intellectuals I comment upon mentors, friendships and those who in some way enabled me to do fieldwork and research in Brazil from 1966 to 2013.

In Part III I have included a series of photos important for the "Photographic Journey." They are scenes one could consider "folklore" or if not exactly that, a scene where folklore takes place or was gathered. In addition I add photos of artifacts of the travels when related to the research. All in all there are fairs, markets and scenes of by gone days which represent places where folklore was found, like the old "Rampa do Mercado" in Salvador and the riverboats of the São Francisco River Company, one of the most folkloric trips in Brazil in its day. As well one sees the leather objects of the northeastern cowboys, the clay dolls of the Caruaru market, wooden carvings from Bahia and anything else which brings to mind the research. Enjoy the photos and memories.

LIST OF IMAGES

"FIFTY YEARS OF RESEARCH ON BRAZIL—A PHOTOGRAPHIC JOURNEY"

PART I. THE POETS AND PRINTERS OF THE "LITERATURA DE CORDEL"

PART II. THE INTELLECTUALS, INFORMANTS AND FRIENDS OF THE "LITERATURA DE CORDEL"

PART III. THE FAIRS, THE MARKETS AND SCENES OF FOLKLORE

THE IMAGES AND THE TEXT

PART I
THE POETS

The poet José Bento da Silva declaiming the poem, the São José Market, Recife, 1966

José was a minor poet in "cordel" in the Recife Market, but the photos are chronological and he was the first poet I encountered. But all this is did not stop him from declaiming a story-poem in fine voice. Note his audience, all male as I would soon discover was the custom.

The poet José Francisco dos Campos, the São José Market, Recife, 1966

Zé Francisco was in the market at the same time, July of 1966. He was a fine versifier with many good story-poems. Perhaps he reached temporary if not lasting fame as a main player in Candice Slater's "Stories on a String" in the chapter "'The King, the Dove and the Sparrowhawk.'"

A vendor of poetry at his market stall, the São José Market, Recife, 1966

This unnamed vendor sold story-poems, comic books and "top hit" lyrics magazines, but he was instrumental in setting up my first opportunity to record a poetic duel ["peleja ou cantoria"] at the old Santa Rita Market near the docks in Recife a bit later.

Singer-Poets [cantadores] at a market stall, the São José Market, Recife, 1966

These are the two singer-poets who will "duel" in verse for me at the old Santa Rita Market near the port of Recife. The duel is described in "Adventures of a 'Gringo' Researcher in Brazil in the 1960s." Trafford Publishing. No photos of the "cantoria" were made.

A poetry salesman reciting a story-poem, the São José Market, Recife, 1966

I was chided by some when I called him a cordelian poet in my book "A Literatura de Cordel," 1973. I guess he just wanted to get in on the action.

The poet Manoel Camilo dos Santos outside his printing shop, Campina Grande, Paraíba, 1966

Manoel was one of the major poets of "cordel" at this time. He is most famous for the cordelian classic "Trip to São Saruê" ["Viagem a São Saruê"] compared by the scholar and writer Orígenes Lessa in a speech at the Brazilian Academy of Letters to erudite poet Manuel Bandeira's "Vou p'ra Passárgada." I paraphrase from Átila de Almeida's Dictionary (the best source for such data): Manoel Camilo was born in Guarabira, Paraíba, in 1905 and died in Campina Grande in 1987. He was originally a carpenter by trade and then began as a singer-poet in the 1930s, an activity he stopped in 1940. His first story-poem of "cordel" dealt with the Missionary Frei Damião. He began printing and selling poems of "cordel" in 1942 in Guarabira, and transferred the shop to Campina Grande in 1953 with the name "The Star of Poetry" ["A Estrela da Poesia"]. He left the shop in Guarabira to a brother-in-law José Alves Pontes, and it became a major typography for "cordel" in the region, providing the printing for many poems sold in the São Cristóvão Market in Rio by his relative Apolônio Alves dos Santos. The Guarabira shop outlasted Manoel Camilo's shop in Campina Grande. Like a few other poets he was "bitten" by the political bug and became a candidate for State Deputy in 1962, but suffered a bitter defeat. His forté was writing entertaining cordelian "romances," the long narrative poems of 32 pages and his memorable back cover tirades against unscrupulous poets and printers who stole others' works, in effect his own. He threated on occasion to unleash his "stable" of lawyers on the "criminals." But "São Saruê was his claim to fame. [Almeida, pp. 411-412]. Átila de Almeida spends a lot of time detailing how Manoel Camilo really got the idea and many of the images from the master Leandro Gomes de Barros in his "Trip to Heaven," ["Viagem ao Céu"]. Be that as it may, the poem plays a major role in our "Portrait."

Curran and Manoel Camilo outside his house-printing shop, Campina Grande, 1966

The poet and astrologer Manoel Caboclo, Juazeiro do Norte, Ceará, 1966

Probably better known for his astrology than "cordel," even though he had some 25 titles to his credit in the 1970s, Manoel had his apprenticeship in "cordel" working in the typography of the famous José Bernardo da Silva, "A Tipografia São Francisco," in Juazeiro in 1938. This author interviewed José Bernardo in his home in 1966, but alas, no photos were taken. Zé Bernardo is famous for having purchased the stock of the great João Martins de Atayde in Recife when the latter suffered health problems in the late 1950s, thus inheriting the huge stock from Recife which included not only Atayde's considerable works and those of poets in his stable such as Delarme Monteiro, but mainly the major works of Leandro. Gomes de Barros which Atayde in turn had purchased in 1921. After leaving the employ of Zé Bernardo, Manoel Caboclo bought a printing press and began to publish his famous

"Almanac," encouraged by João Ferreira da Lima, one of the great cordel-astrologers of the Northeast. And in 1973 he bought the rights to the many story-poems of Joaquim Batista de Sena, a well-known cordelian poet in Fortaleza, and published his own poems as well. Manoel Caboclo thus was a major player in both "cordel" and astrology in the Northeast from his humble surroundings in Juazeiro do Norte, land of Father Cicero. [Almeida, 463]

Curran and Manoel Caboclo e Silva, Juazeiro do Norte, 1966.

**A farmer proudly showing me story-poems of Father Cícero outside
his mud and wattle home near Juazeiro do Norte, 1966**

When asked if he knew of the poems of Padre Cicero, he rushed into his house and brought out a handful of cordelian booklets of verse.

The poet Erotildes Miranda dos Santos, Feira de Santana, State of Bahia. 1966

After taking a local bus from Salvador to Feira de Santana on an incredibly hot day, the author visited the famous fair of Feira, seeking possible evidence of poets of "cordel." One should note that aside from the commercial, traditional fair, the city hosts the largest cattle fair/auction in the Northeast. Erotildes Miranda was the only poet we succeeded in talking to and documenting that day. Not a major poet of "cordel" but with his niche—writing poems of sexual innuendo erotic in tone and at times with photos of scantily clad young ladies on the cover—he was a presence in the fair. "Sex sells," he said.

Singer-Poets [cantadores] at the Fair of São Cristóvão, North Zone of Rio de Janeiro, 1967

On one of my first visits to this famous northeastern fair and gathering place in the north zone of Rio de Janeiro, I documented these "cantadores," unfortunately unnamed. They did immediately begin to improvise verse about the "gringo" at the fair and expected a monetary reward, duly given.

Unnamed poets declaiming the story-poems, the Fair of São Cristóvão, Rio de Janeiro, 1967

Note the use of the microphone to declaim the verse. This primitive system was used in self-defense against the noise of music stands with large speakers blaring out the country hits of the day.

A veteran poet, Fair of São Cristóvão, 1967

This elderly gentleman and veteran of the Fair was one of the first poets to sell the booklets of "cordel" in the market.

The outstanding poet-singer and cordelian poet, José João dos Santos, penname "Azulão," singing the story-poem, the Fair of São Cristóvão, Rio de Janeiro, 1967

Azulão is that rarity, an accomplished poet of "cordel" with well over one hundred titles published as well as a superb singer-poet. Over the years he is perhaps second to none in the poets we have had the pleasure to meet, interview and document. Some of his excellent poems are paraphrased, or selections quoted and/or translated in several of our books.

Born in Cabaceiras, Paraíba, in 1932, raised in Sapé, Paraíba, and arriving in Rio de Janeiro at the age of 17 in 1949, he made a successful career for himself in the big city and in many ways his story is the epitome of the Northeastern Migrant to Rio. Stories like "The Early Morning Train" and "Joe Hillybilly in Rio de Janeiro" are among his classics. We first encountered Azulão singing his verse in the fair in 1967; being a "cantador," he was and still is one of the few who can transport the melodies and nuances of the "peleja" to singing story-poems in the fair. He is shown here with his tiny battery powered "amplifier" and microphone, necessities to compete with the huge drone of noise in the fair. Several more photos will show him over the years with our visits to the market. [Almeida, p. 409]

**A poetry salesman from Belém do Pará selling his wares at
the São Cristóvão Fair, Rio de Janeiro, 1967**

**A vendor of story-poems, comic books, etc. at his shop in
Pirapora, Minas Gerais, along the São Francisco River**

The "River of National Unity" runs from Minas Gerais through Bahia and to the sea at Alagoas. The shop owner was delighted at being interviewed and photographed. His remark I recall, referring to the "cordel: "Brazil has a lot of foolishness ["bobagem"], but some really pretty things as well."

A vendor of story-poems outside the the Ver-O-Peso Market, Belém do Pará, 1967

A vendor of story-poems at the dock in Manaus, Amazonas State, 1967

Manaus is a major river port on the Rio Negro which joins the Rio Solimões and then becomes the Amazon. It is approximately one thousand miles upstream from where the Amazon empties into the Atlantic, the width of the river at that point said to be more than seventy miles. Not a poet, the gentleman received his stock of poems primarily from poets in Fortaleza and Juazeiro do Norte in the Northeast, booklets of verse brought to Manaus by itinerant vendor-poets from the Northeast or even Santarém half way from the river's mouth to Manaus. The poets and vendors in those days traveled on the Amazon passenger boats, the "locals" used by the people themselves, not to be confused with tourist cruise ships which now ply the river.

The poet Apolônio Alves dos Santos, the São Cristóvão Fair, Rio de Janeiro, 1978

This photo has graced the webpage of the U.S. Library of Congress Symposium on the "Literatura de Cordel" in 2011 and the cover of our most recent book "A Portrait of Brazil in the Twentieth Century—the Universe of the 'Literatura de Cordel'". It epitomizes the modern cordelian poet with his stand in the market but harks back to the very beginnings of "cordel" when the poetry was sold in Portugal displayed on a string or a wire in the market by the blind men who sold the poetry.

Apolônio Alves dos Santos was born in Guarabira, Paraíba in 1926 and migrated with the horde of "nordestinos" to Rio, establishing himself in 1950. He came into his own over the years and decades, a regular at the São Cristóvão Fair where we met him for the first time and visited with him on many occasions over the years. There is an old black and white photo of Apolônio with "viola" in hand performing as a "cantador" in the old days in one of Rodolfo Coelho Cavalcante's productions (to be seen later). He wrote dozens of story-poems, many instrumental in telling the story of the vicissitudes of life for the northeastern migrant in the South, but also important stories of life, politics and economics in Brazil in the 1970s and 1980s. He lived in the district of Benfica, a poor district in Rio, really a "favela," and told of the life of struggle and survival there, in one instance being robbed of "a lousy chicken" he was bringing home from the food market. Apolônio after our last interview in the late 1970s returned to the Northeast, but then returned to Rio where he died some time ago. In one sense he symbolizes the myth of "White Wing" ["Asa Branca"], the northeastern anthem by the great forró singer Luís Gongaza. He epitomizes along with many others, including Azulão, the life of the poet in greater Rio. He was a fine poet, good at his craft and published wonderful stories with fine woodcuts illustrating them, poems published by the Pontes Typography in Guarabira, Paraíba. He was one of the highlights of our interaction with the "cordel" over the years.

"Azuláo" singing the story-poem, the Fair of São Cristóváo, 1978

The same small amplifier and microphone of 1967 are evidenced. Note the crowd of fans avidly listening to the master.

"Azulão" in another photo, 1978

"Azulão" at his poetry stand, the Fair of São Cristóvão, Rio de Janeiro, 1978

Yet another photo, this time the poet is preoccupied with actually selling the story-poem and collecting a few "cruzeiros" for his efforts.

"Azuláo" declaiming the story-poem, Fair of Sáo Cristóváo, Rio de janeiro, 1978

Yet another shot, this time with a bird's eye view of the poet in action, singing from the booklet of verse. His vision was failing and the thick lenses and close proximity to the "folheto" are evidence of this. I love this photo; it captures the essence of the poet in the market. Note the crowd he always drew and the hammocks sold in the nearby market stand.

The poet Raimundo Santa Helena, Fair of São Cristóvão, 1978

This poet was a bit of a different personage in the market and cordelian scene in Rio in the 1970s and 1980s. His story-poems diverged greatly from the "traditional" poems: he would publish a "folheto" with six or seven one-page short poems inside with topics that diverged from politics to current events like the AIDS epidemic to the most diverse themes. He was retired from service in the Brazilian Navy and was not a full-time poet. His verse could be acerbic commenting on the polemics of his times—the development of the Amazon by the Military Government or the ecological disasters striking Brazil like the disaster at Cubatão in São Paulo. He is not a great poet, but his "folhetos" certainly marked the times in Brazil.

A vendor of the story-poems at the Fair of São Cristóvão, Rio de Janeiro, 1978

One sees yet another vendor with a hammock stand in the background. It was at this time in 1978 when we believe cordelian activity at the fair reached its apogee, <u>circa</u> 1978.

Sebastião Nunes Batista, Cordelian scholar and researcher at the Ruy Barbosa Foundation in Rio de Janeiro at a "cordel" stand, the Fair of São Cristóvão, Rio de Janeiro

Much more will be said about Sebastião in the section on "intellectuals" to come.

His story is fascinating and important. Suffice for the moment, at this time he is the main researcher and informant on "cordel" at the renowned Fundação Casa de Rui Barbosa in Rio de Janeiro. His qualifications were unique: he was one of the sons of the cordelian master Francisco das Chagas Batista from João Pessoa, Paraíba, a colleague of Leandro Gomes de Barros. Sebastião was a true man of the people, a poet himself, but more importantly a person who characterizes much of the old Brazil of folklore. There is much more to come.

A Vendor of "Cordel" at the Ferryboat Dock, Praça 15, Rio de Janeiro, 1978

We see a vender of comic books, love stories, top hit lyrics magazines and a smattering of "cordel" at the Praça 15 in front of the ferry dock for the Rio de Janeiro—Niteroi line. The photo documents the modest and difficult task of making a living in Rio de Janeiro.

Sinésio Alves, cover artist for Cuíca de Santo Amaro, working, 1981

This phase of photos will deal with the "cordel" scene in Salvador da Bahia. Research will continue after the original 1966 visit to that city. The main poet at that time was "exiled" by poverty to Jequié in the interior of Bahia, Rodolfo Coelho Cavalcante. But research centered on a contemporary of Rodolfo and a competitor, the "Boca do Inferno Popular," Cuíca de Santo Amaro. Cuíca would be the topic of two books by this author, and his story poems documented life in Bahia and Brazil from the 1940s to his death in 1964. Cuíca's poems were illustrated on the covers by Sinésio Alves during this entire time. After Cuíca's death Sinésio continued in his art, among other things, becoming a major artist for carnival decorations in Brazil, particularly at one time doing carnival decorations for the President of Brazil in Brasília. An anecdote of the time was when he told of a major robbery at his home in suburban Salvador when thieves "trashed" his house and car. Sinésio was THE artist responsible for the covers of Cuíca's story-poems from the 1940s to the 1960s, some to be seen later in this volume. Here he is doing a sketch or a caricature, a master of both forms, for the author.

A sketch by Sinésio Alves of Cuíca de Santo Amaro selling his verse

The writer and scholar Edilene Matos with cordelian covers by Sinésio Alves at the "Núcleo de Estudo da Literatura de Cordel," Salvador da Bahia

An example of a cordelian cover by Sinésio Alves, 1

This cover depicts Cuica's "The Woman from Brotas." It tells the true story of a woman who finally becomes so sick and tired of her husband's carousing, drinking and womanizing that one night when he falls into bed in a stupor she grabs a sharp kitchen knife and "liberates" him from his sex organ. The poet would follow with two more stories, one true when the now chagrined husband took revenge, killing his wife in a dark alley in Salvador and another, pure fiction, "The Marriage of the Man from Brotas," when he orders a new "tool" from the United States and it is so large (everything from the U.S. is large) that it causes the plane to crash. Big sales accompanied all three stories.

A story-poem by Cuíca de Santo Amaro, cover illustration by Sinésio Alves, 2

Another example of a cordelian cover by Sinésio Alves, Cuica's story-poem, "The Move from the 'Mangue'." The gigolo is riding in all comfort carried by one of the poor prostitutes of the red light zone of Bahia.

A story-poem by Cuíca de Santo Amaro, cover illustration by Sinésio Alves, 3

This is another wonderful sketch/caricature by Sinésio dealing with Cuíca's poem "The High Cost of Living." All the foodstuffs needed by the common people are seen flying in the sky, their price "out of reach."

Sinésio Alves with a cardboard mockup of Cuíca de Santo Amaro

Sinésio and the mockup of the "propagandist." Cuíca created for the publication of this author's book on Cuíca at the Fundação de Jorge Amado in 1990: "Cuíca de Santo Amaro-Poeta-Repórter da Bahia." There is a documentary movie by Josias Pires about Cuíca which has just come out and is playing in the cinemas of Brazil in 2013.

The common grave site ["cova de raso"] like that of Cuíca de Santo Amaro, Salvador da Bahia

Cuíca died in poverty and was buried in such a grave, but as is the custom in Bahia, a large following group of friends and admirers, including politicians, marched to the grave site.

Maria do Carmo, widow of Cuíca de Santo Amaro, a poor suburb of Salvador da Bahia

The photo is of Cuica's widow Maria do Carmo at the entrance to their modest house in a proletarian sector of Bahia on the occasion of an interview with her in 1981.

Maria do Carmo, widow of Cuíca de Santo Amaro, and their grandchildren

Long time typesetter of cordelian poems, Abílio de Jesus at work in Salvador in 1981

Abílio de Jesus at the Benedictine printing shop, Salvador, 1981

The master typographer Abílio de Jesus is shown setting type for the old press at the Benedictine Monastery in Salvador da Bahia. Abílio did the same task for "cordel" in years gone by. He was an orphan and was taken in and educated with blue collar skills by the Benedictines. This photo shows him practicing the same trade in 1981.

Printing the cordelian poem: type and wood block ["taco"]

The printer of cordelian story-poems Waldemar Santos at his typography in the Pelourinho, Salvador, 1981

Waldemar Santos at the "Tipografia Moderna" in the Pelourinho, Salvador, 1981

Santos printed a colored cover version of the poems of "cordel" of his times, not as advanced as the multi-colored story-poems published in São Paulo by the Luzeiro Press at the time.

**The poet Rodolfo Coelho Cavalcante—the first encounter of Curran
and the poet, the Mercado Modelo, Salvador, 1981**

This was a new phase of research, the documentation of times with the cordelian master Rodolfo Coelho Cavalcante of Salvador da Bahia. Our first encounter after years of correspondence was in the Mercado Modelo of Salvador in 1981. In our first research phase in Salvador in 1966 Rodolfo was "exiled" to the interior, living in poverty, this as a result of spending all his resources on a poets' "congress" in 1955 in Salvador and another in São Paulo in 1960. We did written interviews via the mail and now in 1981 I was in Bahia for live interviews, all which resulted in a major book, "The Presence of Rodolfo Coelho Cavalcante in the Modern 'Literatura de Cordel'" in 1987 by the major publisher Nova Fronteira in Rio de Janeiro (owned by the sons of the infamous politician and muckraker Carlos Lacerda of the 1940s and 1950s).

Born in Cachoeiro do Rio Largo, Alagoas, in 1919, he resided since the 1940s in Salvador. He was a "propagandista" of small circuses in the backlands, writing melodramas for them and serving as chief clown as well. Later he did a short phase as a primary school teacher in Piauí where incidentally he dismissed a young lady student who wanted him to kiss her. His response—if you want to truly be my "disciple" no kissing! He later became a Protestant Preacher for a short while until his definitive conversion to Kardec Spiritism which he practiced until his death. After beginning "cordel" with hand-written poems about the Nazi threat of WW II which he sold in the streets in Teresina, Piauí, in the early 1940s, he migrated, ever so slowly to Salvador, still involved with backlands itinerant circuses.

Rodolfo laid claim to having written and published some 1,700 different titles in "cordel," more than anyone else in its history. Almost all are of the 8 page variety, and many are "homages" or "biographies" the poet writes of local personages expecting a nice donation for the favor. But it is accurate to repeat his mantra—that 50 per cent of his production is moral in nature and the poems have a "moral" message. This is evidenced by his "best-seller" "The Girl Who Beat Her Mother on Good Friday and Was Turned into a Dog," a title Rodolfo claims reached one-half million copies sold over the years. I believe it.

Rodolfo was not talented at writing the narrative tale in verse, the "romance," and he admitted it. Nor was humor his forté. But he was in addition to his moral stories and paid homages, a "poet-reporter" who truly documented the political times. An avowed anti-communist, this because local Communist politicians in Alagoas ordered thugs to tie him up and drown him in a canal because he refused to write a poem extolling their virtues and campaign, Rodolfo never ceased, after surviving, to be an enemy of "atheistic communism" and a spokesman and backer for the Military Dictatorship from 1964 to1985. All can be seen in our lengthy book already mentioned. Perhaps more than any other cordelian poet over the years this author felt privileged and grateful for the long interaction with the poet. He truly believed in the golden rule of Kardec Spiritism—"Love one another."

He was not without enemies who accused him of self-promotion and even having profited from the poets' congresses. One can put such criticism to the side; the poet in effect "went broke" and suffered either sunstroke or a nervous breakdown after the congresses and a humble exile to the interior. But he worked his way back and founded in the 1980s the "Order of Poets and Poet-Singers of the 'Literatura de Cordel'" and convinced the town council of Salvador to provide space and funding for a small poetry stand at the side of the Modelo Market in Salvador, a stand he maintained until his tragic death in 1986. In fact the poetry stand with other poets in charge is still operating outside the Market today.

Rodolfo and his "Golden Medal ["Medalha de Ouro"], the Mercado Modelo, 1981

One of the "manias" of the poet was either receiving awards from admirers, thus the "Gold Medal" shown, or giving out awards himself, mainly "diplomas" to contributors to his many causes. The "Gold Medal" drew particular attention because several cordelian poets of the Northeast wondered what happened to the gold. Rodolfo had to defend himself which he did nicely saying, "What do you mean 'gold'? The gold was symbolic. Since when does a humble poet of "cordel" or a poet-singer have anything to do with real gold?"

Rodolfo and better days, correspondence from the "Núcleo de Cordel," Salvador

Rodolfo in better economic days in the mid-1980s was given a job as an "informant" in the "Núcleo da Literatura de Cordel" in the Cultural Foundation of Bahia thanks to the researcher Edilene Matos. Rodolfo's duties were to welcome researchers, junior high and high school students and the like, and "explain" "cordel" to them. But he was left with plenty of time for his correspondence which totaled thousands of letters over four decades. This was the way he ran his many campaigns, published his private newspapers and did the congresses. We chronicled it all in detail in our book "A Presença de Rodolfo Coelho Cavalcante na Moderna Literatura de Cordel" (Rio de Janeiro: Nova Fronteira, 1987).

Rodolfo with images of the "greats" of "cordel"—João Martins de Atayde, Cuíca de Santo Amaro and Leandro Gomes de Barros

The photo is important because behind Rodolfo are images of three famous figures of "cordel:" João Martins de Atayde, the great poet-publisher of Recife for thirty years from the 1930s to the end of the 1950s, Cuíca de Santo Amaro, Rodolfo's contemporary and competitor in Salvador from the 1940s to the 1960s, and lastly but not least, the greatest poet of all time in "cordel," Leandro Gomes de Barros who wrote and published at the end of the 19th and beginning of the 20th centuries on the outskirts of Recife.

**Rodolfo in the early days, a show of singer-poets ["cantadores"],
possibly José Soares and Apolônio Alves dos Santos**

This rare, old, black and white shot was given to me by Rodolfo. Probably going back to the 1950s he "produced" shows of poet-singers and folklore. He is seen in the background, and the cordelian poet Apolônio dos Santos is the "cantador" on the right. The one on the left is as famous as well. Old timers will recognize him, but I cannot say for sure who he is. I'm guessing José Soares from Recife.

Rodolfo in his home library, interviews with Curran, Liberdade District of Salvador, 1981

Rodolfo declaiming for the recorder, 1981, 1

Rodolfo declaiming for the recorder, 1981, 2

Note the poet with different expressions depending on the spot in the narrative of the poem.

Rodolfo declaiming for the recorder, 3

**Last encounter of Curran and Rodolfo Coelho Cavalcante at his
poetry stand in the Mercado Modelo, Salvador, 1985**

The is the last photo of the poet when we surprised him at his poetry stand in front of the Mercado Modelo in 1985, his latest endeavor being the "Brazilian Order of Poets and Poet-Singers of the 'Literatura de Cordel'." Modest as the Order was, and truthfully it was used to promote the poet's own private interests, it was highly important and symbolic as continuing the presence of this folk-popular poetry in the market where it has been present at least from the 1930s.

**The researcher Edilene de Matos with an old-time cordelian
poet of Salvador, Permínio Válter Lírio and his wife**

This photo is important. It shows the researcher Edilene Matos and the old-time cordelian poet Permínio Válter Lírio and his wife on the occasion of the "50 Years of Literature Celebration" for the novelist Jorge Amado in 1981. Permínio was an active writer of "cordel" in Salvador in the 1930s and 1940s, one of the few who survived those times in 1981. On this occasion he and Jorge Amado sang together the song of protest in the famous peoples' strike again the bus lines in Salvador in the 1930s, the "Circular."

The poet Gonçalo Ferreira at his "cordel" stand in the Largo do Machado, Rio de Janeiro, 1978

This is the poet Gonçalo Ferreira da Silva at his poetry stand in the Largo do Machado in Rio de Janeiro, <u>circa</u> 1978. Gonçalo was just starting out. Through work and friendship with General Umberto Peregrino and his small museum dedicated to northeastern culture in the Santa Teresa district of Rio de Janeiro, Gonçalo "inherited" access to the museum and started his "Academia Brasileira da Literatura de Cordel," a major effort at sustaining "cordel" in the Rio region today. Gonçalo is a fine poet, his forté being political satire. A culminating moment in his career, until now, was the invitation to represent "cordel" at the Symposium on the "Literatura de Cordel" at the U.S. Library of Congress in 2011 where we were united with the poet.

Gonçalo was born in Ipu, Ceará in 1939 and has lived most of his adult life in Rio. He has sold his story-poems in the Largo do Machado, the Feira de São Cristóvão, and now from the center in Santa Teresa.

Several of Gonçalo's poems are quoted in part in our books "História do Brasil em Cordel," "Retrato do Brasil em Cordel," and "A Portrait of Twentieth Century Brazil—The Universe of the 'Literatura de Cordel'" due to important poems treating the economics and politics of late twentieth century Brazil.

A "cordel" vendor in Manaus in 1985

Pedro Bandeira, poet-singer and business man, Juazeiro do Norte, Ceará

Pedro Bandeira, was a well known "cantador" in Juazeiro do Norte, Ceará. He was successful with radio and TV programs featuring the poet-singers. The photo was given to Curran by the poet.

**Curran with cordelian poets Franklin Machado and Expedito da Silva and
woodcut artist Erival da Silva at the Fair of São Cristóváo, 1990**

Franklin Maxado, "O Machado Nordestino," deserves special attention for the role he played in "cordel" in the 1970s and 1980s in Brazil, specifically in greater São Paulo. We were with him several times, generally with his connection to the Fundação Casa de Rui Barbosa in Rio de Janeiro where he regularly provided the latest in cordelian production for the collection of the "Casa." One evening after work he, Sebastião Nunes Batista and I had an unforgettable evening socializing over Brazilian "choppe" or draft beer and I was "educated" about Machado, his life, the "cordel" scene in São Paulo and contemporary Brazil.

Franklin was from Feira de Santa Ana in Bahia and has always claimed that the poet Rodolfo Coelho Cavalcante was instrumental in encouraging him as a poet. Franklin migrated to greater São Paulo and wrote and published, on a shoestring, many story-poems. He battled the old veterans in that city, among them, J. Barros, who considered him a "penetra" or intruder in "cordel" because he had a college degree. Franklin was one of the first, now among many, who would dare to enter the sacrosanct "old world" of "cordel." He was just ahead of the times in the 21st century. Be that as it may, he sold his poetry on the streets of Rua Augusta and at the Praça Municipal in the center of São Paulo to anyone who would buy it. In a way he was a "hippie" poet, dressed in leather vest, round granny glasses and with a beard. He was not a great versifier, but his wit and his knack for social commentary and satire made him extremely popular. He returned in 1990, like many a "nordestino," to his home in Feira de Santana and managed the "Museum of Feira." But several of his titles grace our books, most importantly the satire on U.S. feminism and Betty Fridan and his wonderful satire on "Lampião in the United Nations."

Expedito da Silva was a mainstay in the São Cristóvão Market in the 1980s and 1990s. He entered into our work with an unconventional title from 1984, a story-poem about the famous Roberta Close, the transvestite-later—transsexual Roberta Close who was voted, tongue in cheek, as the most "beautiful woman" in Brazil in 1984. It took a lot of nerve for Expedito to publish the poem. Erival, Expedito's son whom we met just this once, was a promising woodcut artist in Rio.

The singer-poet Téo Azevedo's radio show at "Rádio Atual," São Paulo, 1990

In the 1990s there were several northeastern cultural centers created as gathering places for the literally millions of northeastern migrants to the metropolis. They featured large areas for dancing to the best of northeastern musical artists of the times, including several of the persons in the photo. Radio stations flourished, featuring "forró" and other northeastern specialities such as singing "boiadas" or "cattle calls," and not the least, singer-poets ["cantadores"] whose skills transferred readily to the medium. One such was the singer-poet Teo Azevedo's weekly show in the suburbs of São Paulo. Along with northeastern "standards" from "forró," the most famous being recordings of Luís Gonzaga, Teo encouraged performance of "cattle calls" ["boiadas"] and poetic duels ["cantorias"]. This author was interviewed ever so briefly on this occasion, thanks to a contact by Mike Goodman a fan and producer of a unique combination of musical recording and performance—the blend of U.S. blues and the northeastern "cantoria." Thus the star harmonica player for the "Blues Etílicos" was in the mix and appears to the far right in this photo.

The "Rádio Atual" owner with the famous preacher Frei Damião

This photo was taken of the life-size photo-mural in the lobby of the Rádio Atual featuring the owner on the left, the iconic Capuchin missionary Frei Damião in the center and one presumes, Father Damião's assistant, another Franciscan.

100 Years of "Cordel" Exposition Catalogue Cover

This is Curran's photo of the cover for the "100 Years of 'Cordel'" exposition held in greater São Paulo in 2001. The event covered several months, was extended several times due to its huge success, and literally hundreds of thousands of "Paulistanos" and others came to know of "cordel" and appreciate it because of this exposition. Put together by two influential intellectuals (to be treated later in this book) the excellent researcher Joseph Luyten and a political-cultural icon of Brazil, Audálio Dantas, the event was unlike any other this author has witnessed in Brazil (I was invited as one of the main speakers at a symposium of the event.). Indicative of its importance was the setting—one of the SESC-POMPÉIA cultural centers in central São Paulo; the centers also sponsored big time shows by the leaders of Brazilian pop music of the times, including Chico Buarque de Holanda. The idea was to recreate an actual fair with the poetry stands of the poets; these included the principal poets and poet-singers of all Brazil at that time. But it was as well a workshop where the public could see the poets cutting the "tacos" or blocks of wood which would become the woodcuts that would decorate the covers of modern "cordel." And the poets had the opportunity, since it was a fair, to sell their story-poems and wood block prints—they did well! This icon of the event is in effect a woodcut carved by one of the artists present, Zé Lourenço of Ceará. The event would provide this author the opportunity to meet many poets already known through previous research in Brazil, but also to fill the gaps of luminaries I met for the first time.

The Icon of "100 Years of 'Cordel,'" The "Pavão Misterioso"

This is my photo of the image chosen as the icon for "100 Anos," a woodcut of one of the most famous cordelian story-poems—"The Mysterious Peacock" ["O Pavão Misterioso"] by the woodcut artist Zé Lourenço.

The Icon and Padre Cícero

The "Mysterious Peacock" is in the background and a larger-than-life statue of Father Cícero Batista Romão appears; both were themes for the exposition.

The bandit Lampião and Father Cícero

Artistic wood block print depicting Carlos Magno of "cordel"

This is my picture of a poster imitating the style of the wood block print. It decorated the exposition. The figure represents Charlemagne [Carlos Magno] a main personage in the heroic cycle of cordelian narrative poems transposed from the prose of the European stories into the backlands sextets and septets of verse.

Famous Image of Leandro Gomes de Barros, "100 Years"

One sees a photo of a famous image of the pioneering and perhaps best known poet of all "cordel."

Photos of Cuíca de Santo Amaro and Rodolfo Coelho Cavalcante, "100 Years"

This is a photo taken by Curran of two cordelian masters of Bahia, figures already treated here, the poet Cúica de Santo Amaro and to his right Rodolfo Coelho Cavalcante. This author wrote books on both of these poets, "Cuíca de Santo Amaro Poeta-Repórter da Bahia" (Salvador: Fundação Casa de Jorge Amado, 1990) and "A Presença de Rodolfo Coelho Cavalcante na Moderna Literatura de Cordel" (Rio de Janeiro: Nova Fronteira, 1987).

Cordelian Poet Abraão Batista and his woodcuts

Abraão is a major cordelian poet and woodcut artist from Juazeiro do Norte, Ceará. His works are sold internationally and he has attended international art fairs in Miami and Santa Fe, New Mexico. We have known of his story-poems and fine covers for years and have quoted him in many of our books. We first met in 2001 at São Paulo and then again in 2005 at a "cordel" congress in João Pessoa, Paraíba. Along with poems about the local religious scene dealing with Padre Cícero, Abraão has many important titles on Brazilian economics and politics, particularly when there is a scandal happening. He first caught our attention with his poem "The Uruguayans Who Ate Human Flesh," a true story of survival after a plane crash in the Andes and what it took to survive.

Curran and Abraão Batista, "100 Years"

Poet and woodct artist J. Borges, "100 Years," 1

José Francisco Borges was born in Bezerros, Pernambuco in 1935, began to wrote "cordelian' poems twenty-five years later, and developed his unique style of folk woodcuts. The shop continues today with his children whom he taught the trade active in its production. I think there is a parallel of sorts to Mestre Vitalino of clay doll fame in Caruaru and the many family members who became part of his great success.

J. Borges in a few words is famous, but his roots are in the tiny town outside of Recife, Pernambuco, named Bezerros. We are contemporaries, he starting to write poetry and do woodcuts the same time I initiated research on "cordel" in the mid-1960s in the Northeast.

For some strange reason we did not meet at that time. My first book came out in Brazil in 1973 under the patronage of Ariano Suassuna at the Universidade Federal de Pernambuco, "A Literatura de Cordel." In typically Brazilian fashion, the manuscript was delivered in 1969 and the book came out only in 1973. The cover (seen later in this book) shows a priest holding a chalice high at the consecration of the mass and facing him a holy woman ["beata"] one assumes waiting to receive communion. It is a beautiful woodcut, black with vivid orange background. Little did I know, but it was J. Borges who was commissioned by the UFEPE to do the cover. Sometimes you live right. I have never asked him, but it could be that Borges' woodcut was based on the "miracle" of Father Cícero and the "Beata" Maria Araújo when the host miraculously turned to blood in her mouth—the beginning of the Father Cícero devotion and pilgrimages. At any rate we finally met in São Paulo in 2001.

Borges' works sell from a few "reais" at his local shop in the small town of Bezerros, Pernambuco State, to thousands of dollars at art markets, ateliês and galleries in the United States and Europe. His wood block prints were best sellers for years at the Santa Fe International Folk Market.

J. Borges, "100 Years," 2

Curran and poet-singer Téo Azevedo, "100 Years"

We have already talked of Téo regarding his radio show at "Rádio Atual" in São Paulo.

He has written some "cordel" poems, but they are slightly different from the northeastern style. He hails from Bocaiúva, Minas Gerais and was born 1943. His is a variant of northeastern "cordel" but has its differences as well. Teo himself likes to say that he writes "popular literature from the north of Minas" and the "cantoria" in that area is known as "throwing verse" ["jogar versos"]. The quote is from page 061, Almeida.

Curran, poet and woodcut artist J. Barros, woodcut artist Jerônimo Soares, "100 Anos"

J. Barros is a cordelian poet and fine woodcut artist. In effect he plays the same role in São Paulo as a northeastern migrant poet ["pau de arara"] like Apolônio Alves dos Santos, Azulão or Cícero Vieira da Silva in Rio de Janeiro, although without the considerable "cordel" presence of the latter city. But J. Barros has documented the life and time of the migrants to the huge metropolitan area of São Paulo.

Jerônimo Soares is a half-brother of Marcelo Soares, both the progeny of the humanly prolific José Soares of Pernambuco. We will talk at length about José when showing the shots of his son Marcelo. Suffice to say, Jerônimo is not a cordelian poet but is a fine woodcut artist and his woodcuts grace the covers of many cordelian poems.

Zé Lourenço, woodcut artist, Juazeiro do Norte, "100 Years"

We commented on his talent and the fact he was chosen to cut the iconic image for the "100 Anos" Exposition, no small honor and a good indication of his fame among the artists.

Woodcut artist Waldeck de Garanhuns and his wife, "100 Years"

Waldeck is highly recognized for his work today, an equal among peers of the artists, thus present at "100 Anos."

Waldeck de Garanhuns cutting a wood block, "100 Years"

Waldeck is shown cutting a wood block, preparing what will be the "taco" or wood block for inking and illustration on a "cordel" cover. He is shown in the "oficina" or workshop phase of the Exposition.

Poets Gerardo Frota and Vianna, Joáo Pessoa Congress, 2005

Abraão Batista and his woodcuts, João Pessoa Congress, 2005

José Costa Leite at his poetry stand, João Pessoa Congress, 2005

Born in Sapé, Paraíba in 1927, he has resided in Condado, Pernambuco for years where his shop is named "The Voice of Northeastern Poetry" ["A Voz da Poesia Nordestina"]. He has published hundreds of cordelian story-poems and done thousands of wood cut blocks and prints. He is known for religious stories and commentary on society, but always in a humorous vein. In fact his "gracejos" or humorous poems are among the best of "cordel."

And according to Átila de Almeida he was named among the twelve best woodcut artists of the medium. But he will have nothing to do with political commentary or stories.

We failed to meet him in our first foray to Brazil in 1966, but he did answer our questionnaire mailed to poets from Rio de Janeiro in 1967, writing one of the best interviews which appear in our book "A Literatura de Cordel" and are borrowed by Ariano Suassuna for his novel "A Pedra do Reino". It was then, at the beginning of the military oppression in Brazil that he commented he did not write about politics, "a dangerous plate" in those days. But the aversion to the topic has continued throughout his lifetime.

We finally met in João Pessoa at the "cordel" congress in 2005 where I took this picture. He was still strong, telling his jokes and selling his poems and woodcuts. We had little time to talk, and I think my non-Northeastern Portuguese was difficult for him. But just meeting him was one of the high points of my years of research in Brazil.

José based upon my latest knowledge is still active, writing fine "cordel" poems, doing his own woodcuts and those for others, and actively selling in congresses. In my estimation he is the "dean" of cordelian poets in the Northeast today, but perhaps just an "equal" to the prolific J. Borges in doing woodcuts.

Marcelo Soares at his poetry stand, João Pessoa Congress, 2005.

Marcelo was born in 1955 is married to wife Dina and they have four children. He is probably the "cordel" artist and woodcut artist we know best in contemporary Brazil due the fact we have had quality time together first in Santa Fe, New Mexico, where Marcelo exhibited and sold his wood block prints at the Santa Fe International Art Market a few years ago, and of late, at a "cordel" congress in João Pessoa, Brazil. I helped him accustom himself to the Santa Fe Fair, heard many stories of his youth and life and did interviews with him.

Marcelo told me many things that are not written down, so it is difficult to remember all the details. His father José Soares had three separate families at different times and many children. He was a bit of the northeastern "quengo" or "pícaro" I think. Marcelo remembers as a tiny boy working for his father, riding on burros and then buses in the Pernambuco interior where José would sell his poems in the fairs and markets. It was Marcelo's job to collect the money, give change and keep track of the financial part. José later had a market stand outside the São José Market in Recife where he did a good business over the years. I quote many of his stories in "História do Brasil em Cordel," "Retrato do Brasil em Cordel," and now "A Portrait of Brazil in the Twentieth Century—the Universe of the 'Literatura de Cordel'".

Marcelo is both a poet and a woodcut artist and in 2009 estimated his income was 30 per cent from the sale of "cordel," each story-poem selling for about 1.5 "reais," and 70 per cent from the wood block prints, selling in Brazil for 40-50 "reais." He is well known throughout Brazil, has exhibited in Paris, but perhaps his greatest fame (perhaps unknown by most) was he did all the woodcuts for the set decorations for the TV soap opera ["telenovela"] "Roque Santeiro," a huge hit in all of Brazil via a national TV network. Marcelo has kept in touch via e-mail and told us recently of launching a new endeavor—writer, singer and performer of northeastern music. He said, "I thought I always had the talent, and now have a chance to do it." He has a band that plays at least locally in the Northeast.

Marcelo's base for years was Timbaúba in Pernambuco, almost on the border with Paraíba (he has moved to Recife in recent years). He writes his own story-poems and prints and sells them along with those left to him by his father José Soares, the "Poet-Reporter" of "cordel, perhaps the greatest of all time. In addition some poets come to him to print their poems, so he considers himself an "editor" or publisher as well.

**Poet José Alves Sobrinho of "Dictionary" fame, colleague of
Átila de Almeida, João Pessoa Congress, 2005**

José Alves Sobrinho is a colleague, researcher and principal informant for Átila de Almeida's "Dicionário Bio-Bibliográfico de Poetas Populares," a major source for study of the poetry.

We met José Alves at João Pessoa in 2005 at the congress. An affable gentleman, he was in turn pleased to meet me since I had done a very positive review of the "Dictionary" some years back and he had somehow seen it. Suffice to say, the fieldwork that Zé Alves did was outstanding, an effort faithful to the dictates of Luís da Câmara Cascudo the dean of Brazilian folklorists. The forté of the "Dictionary" is old "cordel" with an emphasis on "cordel" in the Northeast and as well the most famous of its poets. It is as well terrific research on the most famous of the singer-poets ["cantadores"]. The quality of the edition could be better since it was done on a shoe-string, but perhaps the Regional University of Paraíba in Campina Grande will do a finer edition.

Curran, poets and last night out, João Pessoa Congress, 2005

The photo shows Mark, Marcelo Soares, Gerardo and Viana, and an unnamed "cantador."

This was the last night of the congress and my last chance to be with Marcelo.

Marcelo Soares and Curran, International Folk Art Market, Santa Fe, 2009

Marcelo Soares, his woodcuts and Mark, Santa Fe Art Market, 2009

This was a wonderful opportunity to be united with the poet and friend. I was able to assist in the booth and help sell his works to avid customers at the market. One moment I recall was that Marcelo was dying for some "Brazilian Food." None was available at the market but I did find him a facsimile of the rice and beans which are a staple in the Brazilian diet.

Poet Gonçalo Ferreira da Silva, Washington D.C., Library of Congress Symposium, 2011

The photo shows Gonçalo on the Washington Mall on the occasion of the "Cordel" Congress at the Library of Congress, 2011. He lived a very fortunate moment in his career by virtue of being asked by the organizers of the congress to represent all of "cordel" at the event. Having known and admired him over the years and quoting many of his poems in my books, I played the role of "cicerone" or guide even helping him to find something close to Brazilian food, rice, beans and chicken at a local café. But the highlight of the tourism was at the Air and Space Museum in front of the lunar landing vehicle. Gonçalo had chronicled the very event for "cordel" years back. He was beaming!

Poet José M. Lacerda, Belém do Pará, 2013.

I had an altogether too brief encounter with José on Avenida Getúlio Vargas, the main street in Belém do Pará, in October of 2013. He was restocking his story-poems at newsstands along the avenue. His story is that of contemporary "cordel" and the many changes taking place since the "old days" of Curran's initial research. José is from Paraíba state and from his home writes and prints his story-poems. So far so good. What is different is he travels by jet (like any normal Brazilian passenger) from the Atlantic Coast to stops in Fortaleza, São Luís de Maranhão, Belém do Pará, Manaus and far off Boa Vista in the western Amazon to sell and distribute his story-poems of "cordel." This alone marks a significant change in the medium. Only one poet from the "old" "cordel" ever distributed his story-poems as air freight on the old DC—3s of the Northeast, João José da Silva from Recife. But he did not TRAVEL on the planes.

José like others has an e-mail address stamped on the back cover of his story-poems and a web page site as well.

So his, then, is the success story of the contemporary "cordel" in the hectic Brazil of 2013.

Curran and José M. Lacerda, Belém do Pará, 2013

PART II
THE INTELLECTUALS, THE TEXT BELOW
EACH MARKER

This second sector of "A Photographic Journey" treats the folklorists, writers, intellectuals and contributors to the research odyssey in Brazil from 1963 to 2013. Most were in some way related to the study of "cordel" but not all. But they all aided in some way to the success of research and future publications.

Unfortunately we do not have photos of the following important persons: Gastão de Hollanda, Manuel Cavalcanti Proença, Ivan Cavalcanti Proença, Gilberto Freyre, Sylvio Rabello, Renato Carneiro Campos, Átila de Almeida, José Calasans, Vasconcellos Maia, Hildegardes Vianna, Vicente Salles, Renato Almeida, Homero Senna, Orígenes Lessa, and Thiers Martins Moreira.

The Law School, Recife, Pernambuco, 1966

It all started here with this major library. I was sent to the library by the writer and playwright Ariano Suassuna in 1966 because the library possessed the basic and most important books on "cordel" and poets-singers. I spent many an hour sitting in the huge reading room taking notes in lined grade-school tablets on some of the most famous books in

Brazil. One was allowed to get a library card, take the book to the reading room, but not out of the library. And of course there was no Xeroxing.

An aside: I write much of those days in my book "Adventures of a 'Gringo' Researcher in Brazil in the 1960s." Dealing with the poor light coming from tiny bare bulbs far above the tables, the incredible street noise of traffic and blaring radios with the World Cup games on, and the surprising shouts of the street vendors ["pregões:] allowed to come into the library to see their wares, it was a challenge. On the other hand there were the cute young Pernambuco girls about and a new thing for me—the incredibly hot, sweet, strong but delicious Brazilian "cafezinhos" served to the researchers each hour. The work and the reading got done.

Mark and Ariano Suassuna, Recife

One sees Mark and Ariano Suassuna at his house in Casa Forte (Recife) in 1978. I would meet Ariano at his home in 1966. The encounter was short but hospitable, Ariano giving me the tips ["dicas"] for research mentioned in Image 92. But more encounters would come in 1969 when he enthusiastically examined and agreed for the Federal University of Pernambuco to publish my first book, "A Literatura de Cordel" (1973). He in fact handled the proof reading. He later used or borrowed the text from some of the books' interviews for use in his novel "The Rock of the Kingdom" ["A Pedra do Reino,]" something he thanked me for a couple of times later on. Our most recent meeting and most felicitous was at the BRASA conference in Recife in 2000 where he enthusiastically applauded my talk, laughing with me much of the time, of the happenings in those early days of research in Recife in the 1960s.

I cannot tell his story here, but suffice to say, among all his accomplishments, the play "The Rogues' Trial" ["Auto da Compadecida"] is perhaps best known. Written in 1955, produced in Recife and São Paulo and made into a successful film (the top box office film in Brazil in the late 1970s), it was based directly on story-poems from the "Cordel" which I outlined for the book written in 1969. University teacher, famous lecturer with his "show-classes" ["aula-espetáculos"] public servant and family man, Ariano has inherited the role of THE Northeastern intellectual-writer in Brazil. Proof or not of this was a famous samba school featuring him and his career in the samba school parade in Rio some years ago (he was in good company—Chico Buarque de Holanda was another icon so honored).

Ariano Suassuna and his art

Ariano Suassuna and another of his paintings

Painting of friend Francisco Brennand, home of Ariano Suassuna

Ateliê of Tiago Amorim, Olinda, 1966

The photo shows the art studio ["ateliê"] of Tiago Amorim in an old colonial house ["sobrado"] in Olinda in 1966. I write of this place as my first residence in Brazil, albeit a short residency.

Mark at the home of Marcus Atayde, copying Leandro Gomes de Barros' contract with João Martins de Atayde, 1966

A fuzzy picture, but important just the same for this book. Mark is seen sitting at a desk in the house of Marcus Atayde, son of the famous João Martins de Atayde, in a residence near the old São José Market. I am copying by hand and verbatim the text of the original contract of purchase of the story-poems of Leonardo Gomes de Barros by João Martins de

Atayde in 1921, a purchase from Atayde's widow. I was the first to divulge the document in the 1973 book and it clarified much of the history of "cordel" in the Northeast. Many had doubted the legitimacy of Atayde's claim to publishing said story-poems. Atayde was from the 1920s to the 1950s the predominant publisher of "cordel" in all Brazil as well as author of many of its important poems. Marcus would be my guide on many folkloric forays in 1966 including one when he asked me to bring a revolver back to Recife: "No one would suspect an American researcher." Those were dangerous times, but all turned out well. Marcus later vanished from Recife and was said to be "hiding" in greater São Paulo during the military dictatorship. One can only surmise what would have happened had the police discovered the revolver. He would laugh reading this today.

Marcus Atayde and writer Lycio Neves, Caruarú, Pernambuco, 1966

Marcus Atayde would become a good friend and sometime "guide" for my adventures in 1966. He is shown here in Caruraru, my first trip to this important town for northeastern folkore with its market and "cordel" poets, here with writer Lycio Neves.

Professor Juárez Batista family, Joáo Pessoa, 1966

Professor Juárez Batista, Federal University of Paraíba, his family and a young north American researcher. It was Professor Batista who arranged my unforgettable trip to the José Lins do Rego's family sugar cane plantations in Paraíba. And this contact was graciously supplied by my professor of Brazilian Literature at Saint Louis University, Dr. Doris Turner.

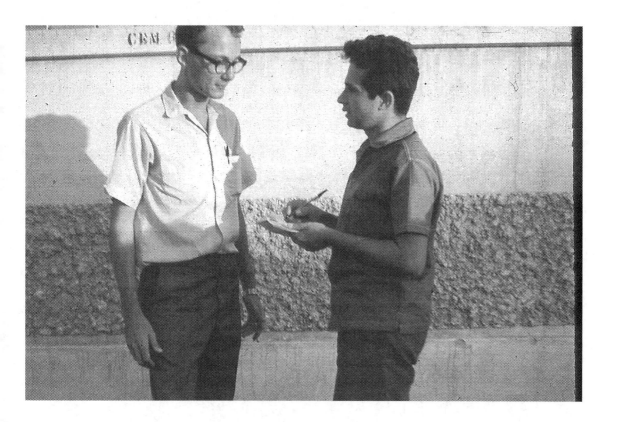

Curran and folklorist Altimar Pimentel, Lins do Rego sugar cane plantations, Paraíba, 1966

Curran and the young folklorist Alimar Pimentel, my guide on an unforgettable trip to the José Lins do Rego family's sugar plantations in Paraíba State. Lins do Rego was one of the "Novelists of the Northeast" with his many stories comprising the Sugar Cane Cycle, sometimes compared to our own William Faulkner in the United States. Altimar in future years would have an amazing accomplishment: the recording of and eventual transcribing of 5000 oral stories to the folk archives of Paraíba.

Folklorist J. Figueiredo Filho, Crato, Ceará, 1966

Professor Figueiredo gave me introductory insights to the Valle do Cariri, Crato and especially the town of Juazeiro do Norte of famed Father Cícero Romão.

Luís da Câmara Cascudo, folklorist, Natal, Rio Grande do Norte, 1966

Brazil's best folklorist received me in his library in Natal, Rio Grande do Norte, 1966. Câmara Cascudo was one of the best advisers during my initial research in Brazil. He not only lived but wrote about the most famous age of "cordel" and the singer-poets. He eventually would write and publish more than one hundred titles on Brazilian Folklore. Trained in History, his interests evolved into both the theory and fieldwork of folklore. His "Dictionary of Brazilian Folklore" is the best of its kind. In addition he was steeped in African Folklore and its evolution in Brazil. He hosted me in a three hour, intensive "master class" at his library in Natal in 1966.

Jaime Pereira Coelho and Flavio Cavalcanti Veloso, friends and folklore informants, Recife, 1966

These two young men became good friends and invaluable informants for my months in Recife, 1966. Jaime introduced me to Campina Grande, his family, his Kardecist father, and most importantly guided me to the part of town and the home of the poet Manoel Camilo dos Santos and later the Campina Grande Fair. Flávio was a general "cicerone" or guide in those Recife days, and his best help was an important example of the Brazilian "jeito." When ready to leave Brazil I needed permission from the Pernambuco Police due to my year-long student visa. The idea was to make sure I had committed no crimes and did not owe any taxes. It was Flávio's intervention, and the "pull" ["pistolão"] of his father Dr. Pedro Veloso, medical doctor, retired admiral in the Brazilian Navy and constructor of the Naval Hospital in Recife that finally greased the wheels for my departure permit. At that point I was anxious to be heading home.

The entire family, "A Portuguesa" Restaurant, Salvador, 1966

This is a photo of the large family who owned and operated "A Portuguesa," the boarding-house and restaurant in Salvador where I was introduced to and really experienced Portuguese language, culture, food and living far from Lisbon for two months in 1966. It was an unforgettable experience each day to take the crowded bus through the hot, humid upper city of Bahia down to the Barra beach, perhaps go for a swim and then experience a little of Portugal at lunchtime. Codfish, filé de mignon, chicken, fried potatoes, rice, beans with ham, terrific bread and a Brazilian fruit dessert were items on the menu. Guaraná, cold "Brahma" beer or cups of Portuguese table wine were the drinks, all this amongst raucous conversation by all. The restaurant was frequented by politicians and government workers from Brasília on projects in Salvador. In addition it was the entry and "home away from home" for the young, ambitious men from Portugal arriving in Salvador to start a new life.

Professor of English and Encyclopedia Salesman from Portugal, Salvador, 1966

Manuel was a Portuguese immigrant to Brazil, seller of Barsa Encyclopedias and professor of English for the governor's wife in Salvador (when he spoke to me in English I could not understand one word). He graciously taught me much about Portugal, this while speaking continental Portuguese. In the background is Barra Beach at high noon, one of the best places to enjoy beach and ocean in Salvador in those days.

Peace Corps Volunteer, friend and folklore informant, Robert Burnett, Copacabana, 1966

Robert Burnett, Peace Corps Volunteer, was one of my guides in Bahia and continued friend. It was a chance meeting with Robert that really opened a lot of doors in Salvador, mainly introducing me to "A Portuguesa" and life there. I owe him much for that. Bob would later accompany me on first forays of tourism in Rio de Janeiro. After serving two years in the Peace Corps where he taught English in Salvador, he returned to the U.S. where he worked for years at the important Institute of International Education in Washington, D.C. A graduate of Stanford, he represented his school well in U.S. public service.

Robert Burnett, tourism at the Jardim Botânico, Rio, 1967. This scene is from the Botanical Gardens with the famous "Emperor's Palms" behind him.

Daniel Santo Pietro, Fulbright Scholar, Economics, Brazil, 1966-1967

Dan and I became good friends during the time in Recife, but were united in trips to Belo Horizonte, Ouro Preto and later Brasília. A Harvard graduate in economics and politics, his project in Brazil dealt mainly with economic development. It was he who taught me much of that reality in Brazil and served as guide-mentor in Belo Horizonte at the Federal University and more importantly in Brasília. Dan remained in Brazil after the Fulbright period working as staff and management for the important CARITAS, Catholic Relief Services in Brazil. One anecdote: on a return trip to Brazil in 1970 with my wife Keah, Dan hosted us in his apartment which we later rented while he returned to the United States to get married. His three inch thick billfold full of government bureaucratic documents and the need for a "despachante" to get them all in order just to bring the new North American wife back to Brazil was a lesson in Brazilian life.

**Reunion, Peter Eisenberg, Columbia University, Daniel Santo
Pietro, Harvard University, in Ouro Preto, 1967**

The photo depicts a reunion with Daniel Santo Pietro, Peter Eisenberg and future wife in Ouro Preto, Minas Gerais. Peter entered the story as a fellow researcher from the United States, I believe on a Ford Foundation Grant to study the sugar cane industry in the colonial period in Pernambuco. His school was Columbia in New York. His was an important topic evolving from the books of Gilberto Freyre, "The Masters and the Slaves" ["Casa Grande e Senzala"]. Peter would go on to write an important book on the topic. I have written of him elsewhere for a couple of reasons: first, he got around Olinda-Recife on a motor scooter ["lambreta"], courageous business in those times. And it always makes me recall one of the best chronicles of the Brazilian writer Luís Fernando Veríssimo, "A Lambreta." Secondly, Peter went with me to an impressive introduction and night at the Afro-Brazilian rite in Olinda, "Xangô." He gave me permission to use the excellent photos he shot that night in black and white in future culture classes on Brazil. His wife was one of those pretty Olinda girls who shared samba, baião and northeastern music with us in "serenatas" on the quiet streets of colonial Olinda in 1966.

Scholars, Rio-Niterói Congress sponsored by the "Casa de Ruy Barbosa," Rio de Janeiro, 1973

The "Casa" would be my future and most important research "home" over the years, the then Casa de Rui Barbosa in Botafogo District, Rio de Janeiro. Ruy Barbosa originally from Salvador da Bahia came to be Brazil's most famous diplomat; he was instrumental in founding the League of Nations in The Hague, Netherlands. Also a politician, he once was a candidate for president of Brazil, but did not win. But he perhaps was most famous as an intellectual, a linguist (polyglot as they say in Brazil), and part of Brazilian hyberbole: "He could have taught English to the Queen of England!" And he was a bibliophile.

Thus when he died leaving his beautiful 19th century home and grounds in Botafogo, it was declared a cultural center, the "Casa de Rui Barbosa." Later it was granted the term "Foundation," an important step in its continued rise in prominence. The main feature is Ruy's original library, both high in quality and number of volumes.

Now it gets interesting. Because Ruy was a linguist, it was decided in the Research Center that it would be important to study not only the nuances of the Portuguese language as seen in the most elite of Brazilian writers, but "popular" Portuguese as well, that is, the language of the masses. And someone suggested what better than the Portuguese of the "Literatura de Cordel?" By a series of accidents, and many things in Brazil come by accident, the Casa funded Professor Manuel Cavalcanti Proença to go to the old Northeast and "rescue" the remains of "old cordel." So with a nice budget he did just that; the result is that the collection of the Casa, numbering today perhaps ten thousand titles, has the best of originals from pioneering poets such as Leandro Gomes de Barros and João Martins de Atayde. The efforts continued in a sub-division of the Researh Center in the Department of Philology under the direction of a Professor of Brazilian Literature at the Federal University in Rio; they involved the first catalogue of titles, first anthologies, and important later studies. Manuel Cavalcanti Proença was aided in the early efforts by a fortuitous team—Manuel Diégues Júnior, nationally known a cultural anthropologist, and Orígenes Lessa, journalist and writer and early researcher and patron of "cordel." This writer arrived at the Casa to consult the collection in 1966 and was persistent in returns many times over the years. I consulted the fragile originals before the Xerox machine, taking painstakingly hand-written notes on the story-poems. Persistence paid off when Professor Thiers invited me to participate in the first book of studies on the "cordel," a work published in 1973. The young Curran was in terrific company: Manel Diégues Júnior, Ariano Suassuna, Raquel de Queiróz, (one of the "Novelists of the Northeast), Braúlio de Nascimento, head of the national folklore center and Sebastião Nunes Batista, major "cordel" informant. The participation opened many doors to future research and publication.

Programa Especial UFF-FCRB
NITERÓI, 12-18 DE NOVEMBRO

CONGRESSO INTERNACIONAL
DE FILOLOGIA PORTUGUESA

II REUNIÃO INTERNACIONAL

The International Congress of Portuguese Philology, "Cordel" Session, Rio-Niterói, 1973

The photo depicts the panel on "Popular Literature in Verse" ["literatura de cordel"] at the 1973 Congress on Camões and Portuguese Philology where "cordel" seemed to be thrown in for good measure as an afterthought.

On the left is my "cordel" guide and mentor over the years from the Casa de Rui Barbosa, Sebastião Nunes Batista. To his right yours truly, then Manuel Diégues Júnior, writer and cultural anthropologist whose son became a major movie maker in Brazil, then Maximiano Campos the head of the Casa's Research Center at the time and then a renowned researcher of "cordel" since 1964—Professor Raymund Cantel of the Sorbonne.

Professor Cantel first came to Brazil in 1964, a bit on the rebound from his original purpose to research Mexico's "corridos" and hearing there of the "cordel." He eventually amassed what many think is among the best collections of the story-poems housed now in Portier in France. More importantly, he was constantly in Brazil over a couple of decades, each time checking in with the press with subsequent articles about him and his quest; he was a bit of the dandy and the fact he was from the Sorbonne did not do any harm. But we owe to him the effort to publicize the "cordel" and its value in the Brazilian national cultural heritage, something that needed to be done. Prior to the "professor from the Sorbonne's" interest, most Brazilian intellectuals, aside from true folklorists, gave little credence to the phenomenon. But Cantel forced them to perk up their ears! He did not really publish that much on the "cordel," but what he did is first rate. It was his appearance in Brazil and the interviews to the press and his talks that did the trick.

Next to Professor Cantel is one of Brazil's truly fine folklorists, Théo Brandão of Alagoas (I place him immediately in line behind Câmara Cascudo as Brazil's best.) We would meet again at the Casa de Rui years later where Théo had amassed a 500 page manuscript on just one traditional story-poem, "The Gambling Soldier" ["O Soldado Jorgador"].

And lastly was a young contemporary, a rising star in Portugal. Arnaldo Saraiva would go on to enjoy a long university career of teaching, research and interest in the "cordel," linking the Portuguese variant with Brazil. To me he was the quintessential scholar from Portugal.

**Scholars Hernani Cidade, Hélio Simões, Segismundo Spina,
and Massaud Moisés, Rio, Hotel Glória, 1973**

One sees scholars from the 1973 congress relaxing in the bar at the Hotel Glória in Rio. The lady on the left was a primary Camões scholar from Portugal (unfortunately I have lost her name). The elderly gentleman was perhaps Portugal's most famous expert on their most famous writer, Luís de Camões of the "Lusiads" fame. To his right was one of Brazil's top researcher's on literature and linguistics from São Paulo, Segismundo Espina.

In the front row on the left is Salvador's top intellectual on such themes, Hélio Simões (I would meet him later at a session of the Bahia Academy of Letters; I had to jog his memory of the young North American). And to his right, not a great picture, is perhaps the top writer on Brazilian Literature of the times, Massaud Moisés of the University of São Paulo.

Same group at Hotel Glória with Mark

I was truly a "young whippersnapper" in those days, but you have to start somewhere! I will write elsewhere details of that Congress, an introduction to the way they do things in the Academy in Portugal and Brazil. It's a great tale. Just one aside: I had a wonderful lesson in the traditional rhetoric of such scholars noting the styles of the Portuguese "predecessors" but just as interesting noting the Baroque rhetoric from Bahia contrasted to the "factual" practical ways of the São Paulo contingent. A final note: Professor Hernani Cidade, upon both of us checking out of the hotel, asks me if he should tip the doorman. He asks me the "gringo"?

Maria Eduardo Lessa, the apartment on Prado Jr.

My delightful hostess, Maria Eduardo Lessa, wife of the journalist-short story writer-member of the Brazilian Academy of Letters—patron of the poets of "cordel" and a writer of seminal studies on them, Orígenes Lessa.

A personal note is in order. Unfortunately I do not have a photo of Origenes. He was one of three or four of the most important advisers for my studies in Brazil over the years. His many studies in Brazil are still important, journalistic accounts of Rodolfo Coelho Cavalcante's congresses and most importantly a book titled "Getúlio Vargas in the 'Literatura de Cordel'." In his later years he headed the "cordel" research center at the Casa de Rui Barbosa. Orígenes possessed, along with Átila de Almeida, the best private collections of "cordel" in Brazil. He always admired my fieldwork and writing, praising it for being straight-forward, jargon free and of great value. This probably explains the free access I had to his collection, valuable for "História do Brasil em Cordel," "Retrato do Brasil em Cordel" and "A Portrit of Twentieth Century Brazil." But it was his encouragement, in tough times for publishing, that resulted in the large book "A Presença de Rodolfo Coelho Cavalcante na Moderna Literatura de Cordel" to be published by Nova Fronteira in Rio, a major publishing company owned and managed by the sons of the late journalist-iconoclast-political muckraker Carlos Lacerda of political fame from the Vargas Era through the Military Revolution of 1964.

Mark, research at the Orígenes Lessa Collection, Prado Jr.

Edilene Matos, Carlos Cunha at home in Salvador

One sees the professor, writer and researcher of "cordel" Edilene Matos and her companion Carlos Cunha, a behind the scenes "maker and shaker" on the cultural scene in Salvador da Bahia.

Edilene and Carlos were invaluable to me in a series of research efforts in Bahia that led to the publication of three books, the first on Jorge Amado, then Rodolfo Coelho Cavalcante and finally Cuíca de Santo Amaro. More importantly, they saved my life socially in many stays in that city, hosting me interminable times for meals, giving advice and encouragement and providing contacts and places for research. And I overcame much homesickness being with them, their children, their tropical songbirds and doggies. I'll be writing much more about them in future books.

Jorge Amado at the Fifty Years of Literature Commemoration

I'll document this event with several photos for it represents still today the most important cultural moment for me in Brazil. After early readings of novels by Jorge Amado in Brazilian Literature classes at Saint Louis University, then an intense period of getting to know Bahia in 1966 through Amado's guidebook "Bahia de Todos os Santos," and continued reading of more of his novels during that year long stay in Brazil, I put it all together in a very modest book "Jorge Amado e a Literatura de Cordel" which by another fortuitous accident brought me to Salvador for the commemoration. They needed a book and mine was available.

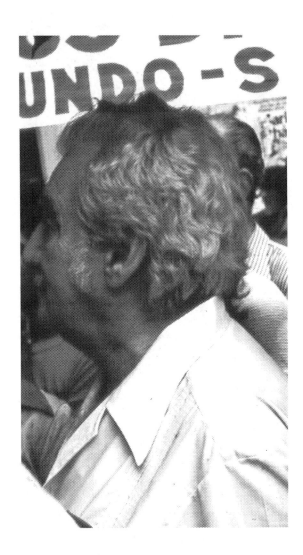

Jorge Amado Listening to Speakers at the "Fifty Years of Literature" Commemoration

Curran and Amado at his home in Rio Vermelho

The photo shows Curran with Jorge Amado at his home in Rio Vermelho. This district of Salvador coincidentally houses the shrine to Iemanjá, Candomblé Goddess of the Sea, where there is a huge anual commemoration to the goddess. I always tell the anecdote: for refreshment they offered me a Johnny Walker Red Scotch and a piece of chocolate cake. I asked Jorge if I was correct in what I said in the book. He said, "Acertou" ["You got it right."] I happily returned to the hotel.

Amado before the commemoration

The Modelo Market was chosen because of its long-lasting fame as a center of folk-popular life in Bahia. The poet Rodolfo Coelho Cavalcante's classic story "A Praça Cayru" of 1943 richly chronicles that era.

Rodolfo Coelho Cavalcante directing, with João Jorge Amado

It was fascinating to see Carlos Cunha coaching the old folk poet to "get it right" for the commemoration: order a big cake, not talk too long and stay clear minded!

Calasans Neto, Illustrator of Amado's books

Calasans Neto of Itapuá, is one of Amado's favorite illustrators and illustrator of Curran's book for the celebration.

Edilene Matos and the Peruvian Vargas Llosa at the commemoration.

Vargas Llosa is one of the major figures of the "Experimental Latin American novelists" of the 1960s, of "Casa Verde" fame, candidate for president of Peru and more recently a Nobel Prize winner for Literature. He was present at the celebration as a reporter for Peruvian television. He was in Brazil at the time doing research for his novel "The War at the End of the World" based on Euclides da Cunha's "Rebellion in the Backlands" ["Os Sertões"].

Researcher Edilene Matos, the cordelian poet Permínio Válter Lírio and his wife

Researcher of "cordel" Edilene Matos with the Bahian, traditional "cordel" poet of the 1930s and Jorge Amado's days, Permínio Válter Lírio and his wife. Edilene would become the principal academic researcher on the "cordel" of Bahia via her link to the Cultural Foundation of the State of Bahia and the head of its "Nucleo for the Study of Cordel," as well as connections at the University of Bahia and the Catholica University of Bahia. She eventually would earn a Ph.D. at the University of São Paulo and move to that city to continue her work. But Edilene became known for her works on Cuíca de Santo Amaro, the "Imagination in 'Cordel'" and general works on "cordel" in the state of Bahia.

**Jorge and Zélia Amado, the luncheon at the Restaurant of
Camaféu de Oxossi, the Mercado Modelo**

Jorge and Zélia Amado are seen at the luncheon they offered to participants in the celebration at the Mercado Modelo Restaurant, owned by Camaféu de Oxossi, a character in many of Amado's novels.

Cover of Curran's book on Jorge Amado illustrated by Calasans Neto

Jorge Amado gives sign of approval to Curran

Gerardo Mayrink, Reporter of "Isto É" at the book signing

Gerardo Mayrink is the reporter of "Isto É" who covered the commemoration and interviewed the Amados at home and later Curran at the hotel in regard to his book.

Calasans Neto at the party

Curran and Zélia Amado at the book signing party

**Researchers Marco Nedú, Sérgio Pachá, Adriano da Gama Kury and
Sebastião Nunes Batista, Casa de Ruy Barbosa, Rio de Janeiro**

This is the research team at the Fundação Casa de Rui Barbosa during my work in the
1980s in Rio de Janeiro: Marco Antônio Nediu, Sérgio Pachá, Adriano da Gama Kury
Head of the Research Center and Sebastião Nunes Batista. The first three were all trained in
Portuguese Philology as befitting that bent of the Foundation. Sebastião Nunes Batista was
different—he was the informant and link to the "literatura de cordel" and served as the main
guide for researchers of "cordel" over three decades.

It is worthwhile to say more about Sebastião. He was a son of the renowned cordelian
poet Francisco das Chagas Batista of João Pessoa, Paraíba, a publisher of "cordel" and a
colleague and contemporary of Leandro Gomes de Barros. There were several sons and
daughters, all who in some way were involved with the poetry, Pedro Batista perhaps the best
known poet continuing a career in Brasilia. But Sebastião's story is fascinating. He migrated
to the Southeast like a good "pau de arara," but took a circuituous route. At one point he

made a living in the interior of Bahia posing as a veterinarian (he had no formal training in that field), but eventually migrated to greater Rio where he became a fixture of the folklore scene. One notable job was as the "the letter writing man" at the Central Railway Station in Rio where he fulfilled the task portrayed by Fernanda Montenegro in the recent film "Estação Central"—writing letters for the illiterate migrants who lived in the poor suburbs of Rio and arrived at the Station to later take buses to different parts of Rio where they served as door men, maids, cooks, and laundry persons. Sebastião wrote whatever they wanted: letters back home telling of the new life and homesickness in the city, letters to old girlfriends waiting for them in the Northeast, even letters of proposals of marriage.

Along with this task Sebastião became a fixture at the northeastern fair in the north zone at São Cristóvão. When the original cordelian reseachers at the Casa de Rui Barbosa, mainly Manuel Cavalcanti Proença, Manuel Diégues Júnior and Orígenes Lessa came to know of Sebastião's great knowledge and his personal link to the masters of "cordel," he was invited to serve in a modest way, and pay, as the official informant at the Center of Philology and indirectly of the "Literatura popular em verso" or "literatura de cordel." He helped organize the large collection, guided researchers (including this author) and wrote seminal studies discovering the true authors of classics of "cordel" which had been lost over the years. Professor Thiers Martins Moreira aided Sebastião and eventually opened some doors for him so that through hard work he earned a Bachelor Degree in Letters at the Federal University in Rio. For years he worked as well as a civil servant in one of the federal ministries in Rio. Sebastião accompanied me many times to the fair, introduced me to poets, and became a close friend and guide in Rio. We sat across the research table for hours at a time, day after day and lunched together. He introduced me to Brazilian "Umbanda" and was my main contact in Rio.

Curran at the "Linguistic Circle," Rio de Janeiro

The "Linguistic Circle" ["Círculo Lingüistico"], Rio de Janeiro. Adriando da Gama Kury was its president and invited me to give a lecture on my research before that august group even though it had nothing to do with Philology or Linguistics. The men accepted me with great courtesy.

The "Linguistic Circle, Rio, famous linguistics scholars

Adriano da Gama Kury and his wife, Botafogo, Rio de Janeiro

Aside from his role as head of the Philology Sector at the prestigious Casa de Rui Barbosa, Adriano was the principal professor of Portuguese at nearby Santa Úrsula University. But it was a "free-lance" position that garnerned him most attention in Brazil. He gave private classes to the elite of Brazilian society to prepare them for the fierce Portuguese language exam at the Braziliian State Department—Itamaraty. And his success rate was phenomenal! He also was a keen fan of Catalán and traveled to Barcelona whenever possible for congresses. He treated me over the years with great respect, corrected and edited my Portuguese on more than one publication at the Casa de Rui, and he and his wife accepted me with great hospitality in their home.

Researcher Sebastião Nunes Batista, Cinelândia, Rio de Janeiro

This was an important moment when Sebastião and I would have a chance encounter with one of the most famous movie makers in Brazil, Nelson Pereira dos Santos.

**Curran, Cinelândio, Rio de Janeiro, encounter with Sebastião
Nunes Batista and film maker Nelson Pereira dos Santos**

Nelson Pereira was a major film maker during the 1960s when the "New Cinema" ["Cinema Novo"] was in vogue. Making movies based on major works of Brazilian Literature, he became known for his "Plantation Boy" ["Menino de Engenho"] by the novelist José Lins do Rego and "Barren Lives" ["Vidas Secas"] by Graciliano Ramos.

Good friends Henrique and Cristina Kerti, Hotel Glória, Rio

Henrique Kerti from Rockhurst days in 1960 inadventerntly was one of the sparks for my lifelong interest in the Portuguese Language and Brazil. Always curious about Brazil while studying for a minor in Spanish at Rockhurst College in the early 1960s, it was Henrique's loud, long-distance phone conversation and the sound of it that added to my interest. His family hosted me upon occasion in 1966 and 1967 during my first stay in Brazil and we maintained contact, off and on, over the decades. His wife Cristina became a good friend as well.

Good friends, Mário and Laís Barros, Salvador

Mário and Laís Barros are long-time Brazilian friends in Itapuá, Bahia; our original friendship dates from Arizona State University days in the early 1970s. Mário and Laís became one of the two main social contacts in Salvador da Bahia from the late 1970s to the new millennium. They as newlyweds were in residence at Arizona State University in those years in the 1970s when Mário earned a degree in Electric Engineering. We maintained contact and continued the friendship for decades whenever I was in Bahia. Mário later became a business executive and free lance broker for economic development in Brazil while Laís with an advanced degree in Psychology opened her own clinic in Salvador.

Most successful student, Roberto Froelich, Rio de Janeiro

Roberto had to enter this chronicle at some point. I've always spoken of him as "my most successful student" from the Portuguese Classes at Arizona State University. He became so enthused about Brazil after visiting the country that he decided to stay and is there to the present. After many years of no contact we rekindled the friendship in several stays in Rio in the 1990s and 2000 where I researched, had fun and mainly enjoyed reminiscing of old times and enjoying the present in Rio. Roberto is a person of significant talents: he is an incredible linguist, reader and scholar of Brazilian Literature and a fine classic guitar player.

This photo shows Roberto putting on a show ["dando um show"] with an improvised concert of classical guitar at a shop in Rio during one of our visits. (I might mention that I played a bit later on at the same shop.) My former student made a living for years teaching English to executives and tutoring the same on the finer points of Brazilian Literature, thus broadening their horizons on both counts. I would like to think I had a bit to do with the latter, encouraging Roberto and other students in the Brazilian Literature classes at ASU to keep reading and to read the masters. He gets an A+. Roberto in later years in Rio would accompany me to the São Cristóvão Fair where I looked for the poets of "cordel," keeping an eye out for my safety and well-being. The student had now become the master—he gently corrected my rusty Portuguese. "Obrigado Roberto."

Scholars Attending the Congress of Northeastern Regional Literature, Recife, 1988

This conference was important historically as an update or modernization of the famous "Regional Movement of the Northeast" in Brazilian Letters by the sociologist Gilberto Freyre in 1926, featuring at that time no less than Jorge Amado, Graciliano Ramos, José Lins do Rego and Raquel de Queiróz. Times had changed and Ariano Suassuna was now the "icon" of Northeastern Literature, but Raquel de Queiróz made an appearance and was lauded by the huge crowd. It was a wonderful moment for this author with a chance to meet her and spend significant time with her.

Ariano Suassuna, Icon of Northeastern Literature

Ariano Suassuna in today's Brazil is the icon of Northeastern Literature and culture. In fact he is one of the major figures in all of Brazilian culture. He became famous for his writings and his administration of important cultural entities in Pernambuco, but also for his marvelous public presence at congresses and in his classes taught over the years at the University of Pernambuco. He had one such moment in his presentation at the 1988 Congress in Recife. He employed a style and technique unique to him: the "class-performance" ["aula—espetáculo"], a rip roaring, humorous and entertaining presentation that wowed the crowds. The technique became his trademark at the University of Pernambuco and other public performances as well as a feature on regional and national television. A minor note: Curran's talk was scheduled immediately after Ariano's presentation, a moment of great humility for the author.

Curran with the famous Raquel de Queiróz, Recife, 1988

As already mentioned, Raquel was one of the four major "Novelists of the Northeast" dating from the 1930s and 1940s in Brazil. She was an icon of Brazilian Literature, and our calm conversations at the hotel in Olinda were important moments in my teaching/research career. It was great pleasure to help her on and off the bus to the meetings and sit beside her on the way.

Neuma Fechine Borges, other scholars, Recife 1989

My friendship with Neuma goes way back to what turned out to be a seminal meeting on Brazilian Culture at UCLA in 1978. (I had recommended her participation at the meeting.) So this meeting in Recife was returning the favor. Neuma was instrumental in founding the major "cordel" collection at the University of Paraíba in João Pessoa. She had a significant link to France and French Literature and in fact garnered her Ph.D. from France. But she became one of the major supporters of "cordel" and its research in the Northeast. She and her husband hosted me at their home in Manira a time or two over the years.

Ronald Daus, Berlin, Lampáo scholar, and wife, Recife, 1989

I met Ronald for the first time at this same meeting in Recife. He was a Full Professor at the University of Berlin and traveled the world representing the university. His study on banditry in "cordel" was done years prior to the meeting, but that does not take away from the excellence of the research; I quoted from the book in my studies. But he admitted he was utilizing free time after this meeting to get to know the "Pantanal" or famous swamp—wildlife region in Brazil's west. At the time it was impressive that he had been offered a position in Latin American Studies at UCLA but turned it down, in part because he was already earning $100,000 per year salary in Germany.

Retired Admiral Dr. Pedro Veloso writing on the patio, Recife home

Dr. Veloso became a friend and mentor because of the friendship I had with his son Flávio during the 1966-1967 year and times later. Not only was he a retired Admiral from the Brazilian Navy, responsible for building the impressive Navy Hospital in Recife, but practiced a traditional Brazilian and Northeastern custom—that of the physician doing journalism. He had a weekly column in the prestigious "Diário de Pernambuco," among the oldest newspapers in Brazil. In addition he had written several books of short stories and a novel or two on Northeastern themes. It was his prestige that through the Brazilian "jeito" allowed me to get exit papers at the police station in Pernambuco in 1967 (proving I did not owe taxes or had committed a crime!).

Director, UFEPE, and researcher Mário Souto Maior, Olinda, 1988

Mário Souto Maior was an acquaintance dating from my initial research days in Recife at the renowned Joaquim Institute of Social Sciences in Casa Forte, Recife, the research center founded and operated by Gilberto Freyre of "The Masters and the Slaves" fame. Mário was a major researcher in Sociology and turned out literally dozens of research articles and significant books on northeastern themes. He welcomed me at his home during this picture and I learned of his major hobby—short wave radio and communicating around the world. Next to him is the then director of the University Press of Pernambuco.

Researcher Liedo Maranhão and Mark, Olinda, 1980s

I had only one meeting with Liedo at his home and library in Olinda, Pernambuco. It was an honor and priviledge for me since he was in fact the major writer on matters of "cordel," the São José Market and folk life in Recife in those years. In particular his study on the folk life of the old market is yet today a seminal work. But his contact with the most important poets and publishers of "cordel" in the region was impressive.

Engineer Flávio Veloso, Olinda, 1988

Flávio was one of my best friends among the university students in Recife in 1966 and 1967, but the friendship was renewed sporadically over the years in my later research or congress visits to Recife. He enters this book because he provided transportation and at times translation in meeting with cordelian poets at the time. He later became an accomplished engineer doing free—lance work at the major sugar cane refineries in the Northeast, much sought after for his expertise. Flávio's family hosted me and wife Keah in 1970 during a wonderful visit and times thereafter. One memorable moment was when they served me a huge crab on a large dinner plate and I simply did not know how to tackle the thing, a funny moment! Another was when I witnessed the still conservative custom of the chaperone in northeastern courtship. I served as chaperone for Flávio and his future wife on an outing— the condition being that I accompany them, and Flávio was about 25 years of age and his fiancée perhaps 22. I presume times have changed since then in Recife, but perhaps not.

"Cordel" scholar, poet, folklore informat in Salvador, Carlos Cunha and Curran, Salvador, 1980s

I have mentioned that Carlos Cunha and his companion Edilene Matos were instrumental in my "cordel" research in Salvador over the many years in the 1980s, 1990s and into the 2000s. This picture recalls the many forays where Carlos would walk rapidly through avenues, streets and tiny streets of Salvador heading to all the second hand book stores where he purchased and traded books. But along the way there were memorable stops and what turned out to be unforgettable cultural moments, i.e. the typographer Abílio de Jesus's work at the Benedictine Press in Salvador, and all the moments of fieldwork and research on the cordelian poet Cuíca de Santo Amaro when Carlos led me to the poet's original residence in a poor area of Salvador where I met, interviewed and photographed his widow and grandchildren and saw the "common grave" sites in the pauper's cemetery where he was buried in 1964. It should be noted that research and collection of "cordel" was Carlos' hobby (he was an erudite poet as well). Both he and Edilene Matos told me that no "self-respecting" writer or scholar could or would ever want to be associated with the "plebian "cordel" in those years. The "Academy" scoffed at such an idea! But his knowledge was a gold mine for me. He was the person "behind the literary scene" in Salvador in those days, a sort of producer of cultural events. It was he who really planned the 50 Year Commemoration of Jorge Amado, along with companion Edilene.

Mário and Laís Barros and Family, Itapuá, 1988.

Mark, Lençois Paulista, São Paulo State, Library, Orígenes Lessa Prize

At perhaps a low moment in my publishing career, it was the writer Orígenes Lessa who encouraged me to enter the contest for the prize. I later discovered that no less than forty essays or works were submitted. My study relating the themes of "cordel" to arguably Brazil's most famous novel, "The Devil to Pay in the Backlands" ["Grande Sertão: Veredas"] by João Guimarães Rosa won! It was not a major thing but did garner me a trip to Brazil in 1985 and I and wife Keah took advantage of the moment to use the Brazilian Air Pass for wonderful tourism in Salvador, Rio and Manaus, a sort of "third" honeymoon in Brazil. Important to say, from that year things seemed to improve and a steady series of publications and books followed, even to the point of this writing in 2013 with a new book out, "A Portrait of Brazil in the Twentieth Century—the Universe of the 'Literatura de Cordel'." I add that it was Orígenes' encouragement that enabled me to persist as a researcher of "cordel." He admired my straight-forward, journalistic style, informative writing devoid of the scholarly jargon of the times.

Mark speaking, Ariano Suassuna applauding, BRASA CONFERENCE, Recife, 2000

This was one of the highlights of the many years of research in "cordel," in effect, recognition of my career work by perhaps the person from whom it meant the most. In my presentation at a "traditional" session, I tore up the "canned" topic and the night before made up an extemporaneous list of the humorous and otherwise "new" happenings and events during that first stay of research in Olinda and Recife in 1966. The speech went over terrifically and Ariano was in the audience smiling, laughing and applauding. It was in a sense his "endorsement" of my work. It was afterall he who had mentored me in 1966, directing me to the Law School Library to read the major works on "cordel" and who sponsored my first book in Brazil in 1973.

Zélia and Ariano Suassuna and Mark, Recife, 2000

Related to the earlier moment, it was at lunch after the session that Ariano pulled me aside and gave a sincere thank you for allowing him to use the interviews of the poets from my 1973 book as dialogue for his major chacter, the poet Quaderna, in his novel "Romance of the Rock of the Kingdom" ["Romance da Pedra do Reino"]. Upon reflection, I wonder if his active sponsorship of the book was due to the section with interviews on the poets, or perhaps the chapter where I delineated his use of the "cordel" in his play "The Rogues' Trial" Perhaps that fed his enthusiasm, perhaps already thinking of those interviews. At any rate, I am just happy to be able to be associated a bit with this icon of Brazilian Literature and Northeastern Culture.

Zélia and Ariano Suassuna, Recife, 2000

Audálio Dantas, São Paulo, 2001

In 2001 I was introduced to another icon of Brazil, but this time a man of journalism and national politics. Audálio was the curator for the "100 Years of 'Cordel'" Exposition at the SESC-POMPÉIA pavilion in São Paulo, an event written of in Part I The Poets. He would treat me with great respect and a mutual friendship would develop, much enlarged upon in 2002 when I returned to São Paulo. His importance in Brazil in the Twentieth Century cannot be underestimated, and we "clicked." I wrote in 2002 that this was the person I enjoyed most in all my years in Brazil.

Audálio first garnered fame in Brazil through courageous and high quality journalism, writing for major dailies as well as in-depth reports for national reviews like "Realidade." He was instrumental in reporting the inframous Vladimir Herzog case of military torture and death of a São Paulo journalist, risking his own life as well. He was the journalist who aided the "favela" liver and "garbage dump collector" ["cata lixo"] in getting her story into print, the diary of a "favelada" which excited sociologists throughout the world. I speak of "Carolina de Jesus" and her book "Quarto de Despejo."

One of Audálo's outstanding articles for "Realidade" was an in-depth story of the wood burning sternwheelers on the São Francisco River in Minas Gerais and Bahia (we shared this experience). In a special report on the Cuba of Fidel Castro Audálio told me of all the foreign press being herded into a Havana hotel ballroom at ten p.m., waiting about four hours for Fidel's arrival, his arrival and first move to take off his pistol and belt and put them on top of a piano and proceed to rant and rave for five hours to the press.

Audálio became the head of the Association of Journalists of São Paulo and was later elected to the Brazilian House of Representatives by the MDB party. In later years he continued to write, including major books on Graciliano Ramos, and did free lance work, including curating the "100 Years'" Festivities. He was kind to this author and we really were on the same wave link—he was and is an important part of our life and research in Brazil.

Joseph Luyten and his library, São Pauo, 2001

Joseph Luyten, originally from Holland and an immigrant to Brazil, became one of "cordel's" top notch researchers and certainly its most meticulous! We had a long correspondence over two decades before finally meeting at the "100 Years of 'Cordel'" Exposition in São Paulo in 2001. Joseph along with curator Audálio Dantas organized the massive Exposition. He and his wife Sônia hosted me during those days.

Joseph figures in all the major bibliographies on "cordel," and in fact compiled the best! His collection of "cordel" was astounding, the only researcher I knew who not only collected thousands of cordelian story-poems but editions of the same! As well he collected folk-popular poetry from all over the world and all the secondary works. His gift to me was a Xerox copy of the original work in prose, "Carlos Magno e os 12 Pares da França," a seminal text in prose from the Garnier Bookstore in Rio de Janeiro and THE primary source the pioneering poets like Leandro Gomes de Barros converted to verse in the early extant cordelian romances in the Northeast. I was once again astounded to see his files on research, correspondence over the years (he had a thick file just of our correspondence), and related matters.

Among other feats, he was also instrumental in introducing and writing of the "cordel" in one of his tenures in Japan (his wife Sônia became renowned as a scholar on Japanese "Manga"). But his crowning achievement was providing the rare cordelian poems for the Exposition in 2001 as well as coordinating the event along with Audálio Dantas.

He died of complications of a stroke a year or two after the event. I was indeed privileged to be a friend and admirer.

Assis Angelo, São Paulo, 2002

Assis Angelo is a television-radio personality in greater São Paulo with the major program on northeastern culture in the huge city. His late night TV show with up to date email and texting components reaches an audience of more than a million. By virtue of this author's long-standing research in the Northeast we had a fine encounter at Assis' residence which is a sort of mini-museum of the Northeast.

Rosilene, (Zé Bernardo Scholar) and Ivone Maia (FCRB) João Pessoa, 2005

These ladies are important figures in research on the "cordel." Rosilene did her master's thesis on José Bernardo da Silva and his printing shop "A Typografia São Franisco" in Juazeiro do Norte, Ceará. We spoke of Silva's importance in "cordel" in Part I of this book. By purchasing the stock of an ailing João Martins de Atayde in the late 1950s, he also "inherited" the stock of Leandro Gomes de Barros, and in effect, became the largest printer of "cordel" in all Brazil at that time. She was happy to meet me because I actually met HIM in 1966.

Ivone did a much more behind the scenes task, but no less important. She was the main person in charge of the digitalizing of the "Leandro Gomes de Barros" "cordel" collection, and for that matter, the organization for future digitalizing of the entire Fundação Casa de Rui Barbosa collection of "cordel" in Rio de Janeiro. After corresponding with her for a year or two we finally had the opportunity to meet in João Pessoa in 2005.

**Portuguese scholar, writer from O Porto, Arnaldo Saraiva
improvises on the bus. João Pessoa, 2005**

Perhaps it is fitting to end this section of "A Photographic Journey" with this photo of Arnaldo because in a sense it both marks the near beginning and end of my research in Brazil. Although not close friends, we became acquaintances and long-time research associates. The friendship dates to 1973 when we both as very young scholars participated in the 1973 Congress of Portuguese Philology in Rio de Janeiro. Arnaldo was taking the tack of researching the roots of the Brazilian "cordel" in Portugal (where he has had a marvelous career as a professor at the University of Portugal in O Porto) while I was working on the Brazilian phenomenon, in particular at that time, the works of its seminal poet Leandro Gomes de Barros. This photo showed a wonderful non-scholarly side of Arnaldo improvising his own hilarious verse and stories on the bus returning from Campina Grande in Paraíba to João Pessoa.

PART III
FOLKLORE, FAIRS AND SCENES
OF FOLKLORE

The Fair of Caruarú, Pernambuco, 1966

The photo shows a "matuto" or country person in his leather sandals or "alpargatas" in front of the merchants. Also seen are huge bags of rice and manioc flour.

Ceramics, Clay Dolls, Fair of Caruarú, 1966, 1

The famous clay dolls ["bonecos de barro"] of the Caruarú Fair, 1966. It was at this time that the dolls became well known, first of all because of "Master" Vitalino, and then after his death, his family. The dolls were of extremely humble origin. They were exactly what they say: dolls for little children made out of clay, rolled, formed, baked and sold. The advantage: if you dropped one, you easily made another. So this was in its essence pure "folklore" of the Northeast. But artists, art galleries and the press caught on and "Master" Vitalino became famous in Brazil. Eventually the dolls could be found in the stores of the major airports of Brazil, in the show windows ["vitrines"] at the side of Rio's Othon Palace Hotel in Copacabana and elsewhere. This author followed the evolution of the craft, from small town rural fair to this tourist phenomenon. It was said that Vitalino made no money from it all and that it was a classic example of the exploitation of the poor by the rich. "Azulão" in a cordelian poem points out this exploitation of the clay doll artist as well as his own.

Clay Dolls, Fair of Caruarú, 2

The dolls in this picture of 1966 show the themes relevant to the times: the bandits Lampião and Maria Bonita, St. Francis and various scenes of the Northeast.

Clay Dolls, Fair of Caruarú, 3

A close up of the dolls in 1966; note that few are painted. Here one sees the bandit Lampião and other figures.

Curran's Collection, Clay Dolls 1

These clay dolls are of a more recent vintage: they show the back lander lady with her goat, the scene of "migrants" ["retirantes"] fleeing from the drought, and on the right, the back lander marriage with the groom carrying the bride off on his trusty steed.

Curran's Collection, Clay Dolls 2

This scene shows two groups of northeastern musicians. St. Francis and his birds are on the right.

Curran's Collection, Clay Dolls 3

These dolls from Curran's collection show the famous bulls and the northeastern cowboy ready to grab the bull's tail and bring it down. See the story-poem of the "Mysterious Bull" for such scenes.

Curran's Collection, Clay Dolls 4

This scene shows the Northeastern musicians and all their instruments. In 1966 these dolls were not painted but were in the color of the original clay.

Northeastern Cowboy, Knight of the Backlands

This is friend Jaime Pereira Coelho dressed resplendently in the legitimate outfit of the classic northeastern cowboy: leather boots, leggings, vest, jacket, gloves and cowboy hat. Although it may seem extravagant, this outfit was legitimate in the 19th and 20th century backlands "sertão" of Brazil and remained as an iconic image of the same. Such apparel was useful when cowboys rode their horses through brambles and thorns in pursuit of fleeing bulls. Such cowboys became known as the "knights of the backlands."

Leather Cowboy Hat, Vest and Gloves

**Northeastern Cowboy Hat, Statue of Father Cícero, Rosewood
Statues of Maria Bonita and Lampião**

Nothing better could exemplify the folklore of the Northeast.

Wood block print, "Northeastern Rodeo," by Marcelo Soares

Fair of Juazeiro do Norte, Man in White Linen Suit

This is a wonderful image of the fairs of the interior of Brazil in 1966. The buyer is in a white linen suit (a custom brought by the English to northeastern Brazil in the 19th century, possibly a vestige of the clothing needed in the Empire in tropical Africa and India and then Brazil), but ironically here is a peasant seeking to buy the "hard sugar cane candy-sweetener" ["rapadura"] of the fairs of the Northeast.

Fair of Juazeiro do Norte, Beans and Rice for Sale

Fair of Juazeiro do Norte, Sugar Cane Block Sweet ["rapadura"] for Sale

Wood Block Print, "Cutting the Cane," by Marcelo Soares

The photo is yet another marvelous depiction of a common northeastern reality: the cutting of the sugar cane.

Ritual of Xangô Initiation

The photo shows the entry way to a center of worship of the Xangô African-Religious cult in Recife.

Pai de Santo, Xangô Initiation, Recife, 1966

The "Father of the Saint" [Pai do Santo] begins the cult of initiation of one of the "daughters of the saint." She would be dressed in white, with the blood of chickens streaming down her face, the feathers of the same stuck on her face, neck and body, all a part of the purification ceremony in this temple of Xangô on the outskirts of Recife.

The Market Ramp, Salvador, 1966

In the 1960s this author purchased Jorge Amado's "Bahia de Todos os Santos," his guidebook to the city of Salvador, Bahia (the first edition was 1944 and he updated and enlarged it over the years). I made it a priority to see everything Amado talked about in the book. His novels of popular life in the city are still entertaining, among them "Mar Morto" or "Death and the Death of Quincas Wateryell" or even "Dona Flor and Her Two Husbands." The folk life at the bay's edge in the lower city on the docks next to the Modelo Market was an important scenario. These scenes have all disappeared in today's Salvador. The area was "cleaned up" for the tourists; the market ramp is gone as is the fish market to its side and most importantly the small sail-cargo boats, the "saveiros." These photos show how it was in 1966 when the area was an integral part of Bahia's folk-popular life. This first photo shows vendors at the market ramp.

The Fish Market at the Market Ramp, Salvador

Classic "Saveiro," Market Ramp, Salvador, 1966

We see the classic "saveiro" or cargo-passenger-sail boat in the bay. Amado wrote fiction of the boatmen who would occasionally save the lives of drowning passengers from transatlantic ships in storms in the bay, but mainly he wrote of the food, work, partying and loving that took place by such sailors.

Ocean Liner in the Distance Recalls Jorge Amado's "Mar Morto"

The whiteness of the transatlantic passenger ship in the distance at dawn in the Bay of Salvador de Todos os Santos brings to mind talk I heard from the poor workers watching the ship come in: "What luxury!" or "Terrific; lots of good looking white girls on that one."

The "Saveiro" Dock, 1966

One sees the flurry of activity and commerce at the "saveiro" dock to the side of the Modelo Market, 1966.

Unloading, Classic Scene at "Saveiro" Dock, Salvador, 1966

This is one of my favorite photos which show life as it was in the 1940s, 1950s and 1960s in Salvador.

Fair of Água dos Meninos, Salvador, 1

The other main place to see the "saveiros" and the resulting huge market was at the Fair of "Água dos Meninos" [The Boys' Beach]. This was a sprawling affair in 1966 and was then the major outdoor market for foodstuffs and folk life in Salvador. The site was depicted in Jorge Amado's "Death and the Death of Quincas Wateryell" and was the scene of the card games of one its main characters "Private Martín" ["Cabo Martin"].

Fair of Água dos Meninos, Salvador, 2

One sees the "saveiros" and the market stands of the fair.

Fair of Água dos Meninos, 3

The picture shows crowds at the market. The Água dos Meninos market burned down a few years ago; it has been replaced by the Fair of São Jerônimo, but without the bay and the boys swimming in the water. All merchandise arrives now by truck and "kombi" or van.

Fair of Feira de Santana, Bahia State, Woman and Cigar

The fair of Feira de Santana, Bahia, is some two hours by bus into the interior from Salvador. The author found "cordel" poets here in the crowded, hot market. Here he caught a lady returning change from her snazzy white purse while smoking a cigar.

The Shoemaker Manoel and his Wife Maria, Salvador, 1966

The shoemaker Manoel and his wife Maria showed me incredible hospitality, welcoming me into their modest home where they served a plentiful "almoço" or big lunch, spending, I surmise, at least a week's food budget. All took place because of a word of introduction by my professor of Portuguese and Brazilian Literature at Saint Louis University, Dr. Doris Turner.

The Heads of Lampião, Maria Bonita and other "Cangaceiros," Nina Rodrigues Museum, Salvador

I saw the heads of the famous bandit Lampião, his consort Maria Bonita, the famous bandit Corisco and others in jars of formaldehyde in the Nina Rodrigues Museum at the side of the School of Medicine of Bahia, a renowned institution of past centuries. It was surmised by the then positivist school of thinking that an examination of the craniums might reveal the "cause of banditry." The heads remained from 1938 the year of the bandits' death until the late 1960s or 1970s when public outcry finally caused them to be buried. These figures are central to the story-poems of the "literatura de cordel."

Weaving of "Bahianas" by Kennedy

This is a beautiful commercial weaving of stylized Bahian ladies by the artist Kennedy, a splurge purchase by the author in a moment of great enthusiasm. Today I have no regrets. It is a wonderful souvenir of my many stays in Salvador.

Wood Carving of "Capoeira," Bahia

This is a wood carving depicting the self-defense-dance in Salvador. The dance is often done in the streets or at fairs or markets, in this case in front of one of the churches of the city.

Wood Carvings, Bahia

Wood carvings from Bahia depicting a Bahian lady in all her finery with a basket of fruit on her head (the stereotyped image depicted by Carmen Miranda of Brazilian musical fame), a fisherman drawing in his net after a successful catch and a colonial façade in old Salvador.

"Caldo de Cana," Fair of São Cristóváo, Rio de Janeiro, 1967

"Caldo de cana" or "green sugar cane drink" is a mainstay at the markets visited by northeasterners, either in the northeast or at fairs or markets in the southeast in Rio or São Paulo. The scene shows one man trimming the stalks of sugar cane and another feeding them into the grinder which produces the thick, viscous liquid. This author did not care for the stuff. The scene is from the Fair of São Cristóváo in the north zone of Rio de Janeiro in the 1960s.

Blind Sound Box Player, São Cristóváo, 1967

A blind, sound box player is seen entertaining the crowd at the same fair in the north zone of Rio. In those days "forró" or northeastern music was just coming into its own. Long the favorite music of the northeasterners, in the 1970s and 1980s it was hugely popularized by musicians like Luís Gonzaga (and the movie "Bye Bye Brasil"). Dance halls with a northeastern theme rose up all over Brazil. The more modest trios had existed for years prior to the burst of popularity.

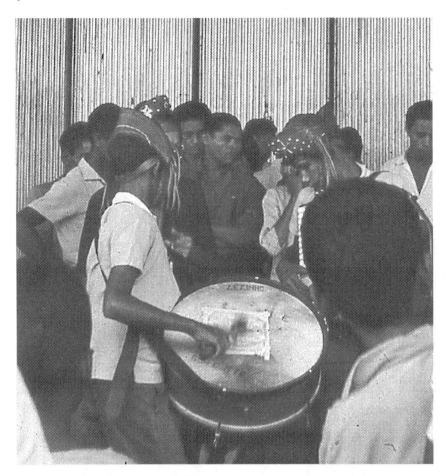

Northeastern Trio, "Forró" Music, São Cristóvão, 1967

A modest "forró" trio at the side of pavilion at the Fair of São Cristóvão. The instruments were triangle, sound box (a type of accordion) and drums. The leather northeastern cowboy hats were mandatory dress, but this modest trio in no way matched the "TV glamor" of the full outfits of singers like Luís Gonzaga (I compare the latter's outfit to Roy Rogers' outrageous embroidered, fringed shirts in his movies, or even worse, Porter Wagoner's outfits at the Grand Old Opry). "Forró" blasts today from many music stands with huge speakers and "forró" cafés at the market. I've left the Fair many times with a splitting headache resulting from the ubiquitous Brazilian custom of playing music at an insane volume. The unfortunate "cordel" poets trying to sing their story-poems in a wonderful folkloric performance at the fair have adopted microphones and small p.a. systems themselves just to be heard and compete. But they are losing the battle.

Riverboat, São Francisco River, 1967

A classic sternwheeler from the São Francisco Navigation Company on the São Francisco River in Minas Gerais and Bahia states in the 1960s. These wood burning sternwheelers navigated the river as regular passenger—freight carrying boats up to the late 1960s or early 1970s. Some came from the Rhein in Germany, others from the United States but others were constructed in Brazil. That is all a thing of the past now except for one tourist boat. I described the journey in great detail in my book "Adventures of a 'Gringo' Researcher in Brazil in the 1960s." The downstream trip took 14 days from Pirapora, Minas Gerais State, to Joaseiro da Bahia. It was indeed folkloric with an interesting cast of characters—riverboat captains, ruddy crew, and passengers including a woman who walked on her knees from the dock at Bom Jesus da Lapa to the shrine, a scary, beer-drinking, gun toting cattleman who said he could swim across the river with me on his back, and finally a grizzled prospector who tried to sell me his semi-precious stone mine in Bahia. Its most folkloric stop was at the shrine in the town of Bom Jesus da Lapa.

Canoe, São Francico River, 1967

A small canoe with freight. This is the type immortalized in a short story by Brazil's novelist João Guimarães Rosa; the same author wrote arguably Brazil's best modern novel, "The Devil to Pay in the Backlands" ["Grande Sertão: Veredas"] in 1956.

Sternwheeler with Cotton Cargo, São Francisco River, 1967

This is one of the sternwheelers with its cargo of cotton bales (and below deck huge glass jugs of sugar cane rum ["cachaça]) headed upriver to Pirapora. The rum would end in the stores and bars of Belo Horizonte, Rio or São Paulo.

Ver-O-Peso Market, Belém do Pará, Vultures and Fishing Boats, 1967

Another of the famous markets in Brazil, the Ver-O-Peso ["Check the weight"] in Belém do Pará. I interviewed folk poets there in 1966, returned with wife Keah in 1970, and saw the remodeled but much less folkloric market again in 2013 while on staff on the Lindblad-National Geographic Expedition to South America.

Icing Down the Fishing Boats, Ver-O-Peso

Icing down the small fishing boats at the Ver-O-Peso; I noted the workers wore no shoes. This was of significance to me because I worked in an ice plant in Abilene, Kansas, while a teenager, the same plant where President Dwight D. Eisenhower worked a bit as a young man. We wore heavy work boots, taking into account the 300 pound cakes of ice.

Market at the Docks, Rio Negro, Manaus, 1967

Passenger Boats at the Dock, Manaus, 1967

The many passenger boats at the docks of Manaus; there are the "ferries" of major and minor rivers in the great Amazon Region, including the Rio Negro, the Solimões, the Amazon and many tributaries as far as Colombia and Peru.

River Boats at the Dock, Manaus, 1967

End of Day, "Jangada" Fishing Boats, Fortaleza, 1967.

Lone Fisherman, "Jangada" Beach, Fortaleza, 1967

EPILOGUE

Thus concludes this gallery of the photographic journey. At this juncture I think it will serve mainly as a nice memory for me recalling all the years immersed in Brazil's folklore, meeting its cordelian poets and publishers, and being with the intellectuals and friends linked to all this. But also I believe these black and white photos, not all but most, serve an important purpose as a visible record of people and times gone by in a Brazil that was, in a few words, more "folkloric." What is certain is that many depict people and scenes now disappeared in the hustle and bustle of Brazil in the twenty-first century.

ABOUT THE AUTHOR

Mark Curran is a retired professor from Arizona State University where he worked from 1968 to 2011. He taught Spanish and Brazilian Portuguese languages and their respective cultures. His research specialty was Brazil's folk-popular literature or as it is known in Brazil, the "literatura de cordel," and he has published many research articles and eleven books on the subject in Brazil, the United States and Spain. Subsequent books are mainly autobiographical and/ or reflect civilization classes taught at ASU: the series "Stories I Told My Students."

Published Books

A Literatura de Cordel. Brasil. 1973.

Jorge Amado e a Literatura de Cordel. Brasil. 1981

A Presença de Rodolfo Coelho Cavalcante na Moderna Literatura de Cordel. Brasil. 1987

La Literatura de Cordel—Antología Bilingüe—Español y Portugués. España. 1990

Cuíca de Santo Amaro Poeta-Repórter da Bahia. Brasil. 1991.

História do Brasil em Cordel. Brasil. 1998

Cuíca de Santo Amaro—Controvérsia no Cordel. Brasil. 2000

Brazil's Folk-Popular Poetry—"a Literatura de Cordel"—a Bilingual Anthology in English and Portuguese. USA. 2010

The Farm—Growing Up in Abilene, Kansas, in the 1940s and the 1950s. USA. 2010

Retrato do Brasil em Cordel. Brasil. 2011

Coming of Age with the Jesuits. USA. 2012

Peripécias de um Pesquisador "Gringo" no Brasil nos Anos 1960, ou, À Cata de Cordel. USA. 2012

Adventures of a 'Gringo' Researcher in Brazil in the 1960s. USA, 2012

A Trip to Colombia—Highlights of Its Spanish Colonial Heritage. USA, 2013

Travel, Research and Teaching in Guatemala and Mexico—In Quest of the Pre-Columbian Heritage, Volume I—Guatemala, Volume II—Mexico. USA, 2013

A Portrait of Brazil in the Twentieth Century—The Universe of the "Literatura de Cordel."
   USA, 2013
Fifty Years of Research on Brazil—A Photographic Journey. USA, 2013

Professor Curran lives in Mesa, Arizona, and spends part of the year in Colorado. He is married to Keah Runshang Curran and they have a daughter Kathleen who lives in Albuquerque, New Mexico. Her documentary film <u>Greening the Revolution</u> was shown most recently at the Sonoma Film Festival. Katie was named "Best Female Director" at the Film Festival in Oaxaca, Mexico.

The author's e-mail address: <u>profmark@asu.edu</u>
His website: http://www.currancordelconnection.com